# Secret Business Growth Strategies

A Business Owner's Guide to Doubling Annual Revenue from $1 Million to $2 Million while Massively Increasing Profitability

An About to Fly Business Book by

# Michael Guy Clark

# Publishing History

**Kindle Edition 1 / November 2018**
ASIN: B07KPBM1XJ

**Paperback Edition 1 / November 2018**
ISBN-13: 9781731599094

All Rights Reserved.

## Copyright @ 2018 Michael Guy Clark

I wrote this book to make your life easier and you're welcome to share the love. Feel free to pass it on to others, share it, photocopy it, stick it on your wall, put it on your Facebook account, etc., etc. My only request is that when you share these ideas and insights. Let people know where the good ideas came from.

**No-Brainer Disclaimer:**

This is a book of helpful, general advice. Like all general advice, expect it to be helpful a lot of the time, but never, ever make significant business decisions in your own business without chatting with the experts who specifically know your business inside and out. I take no legal responsibility for decisions that you make in your business. Use your brain, get good, independent advice and give it your best shot.

# Books by Michael Guy Clark

**About To Fly Business Books**

You're a Business Owner, Not a Slave – 2018

Secret Business Growth Strategies – 2018

# Table of Contents

Don't End Up in an Ambulance ............................................. 1

Is Your Business Built For Growth? ...................................... 4

Keeping Profitability High ..................................................... 7

The Five Big Profitability Levers ........................................ 10

Hit the Right Level of Quality ............................................. 24

Systematise Everything ...................................................... 29

Outsource like a Master ...................................................... 40

Winning Mindsets, Goal Setting, Balance and More ........ 52

Rethinking Minimum Viable Product ................................ 59

How to Spend Your Work Time for Best Growth and Profitability ........................................................................... 62

Leading and Managing Staff .............................................. 70

Mastering Company Culture and Health .......................... 76

Consulting is Like Steroids ................................................ 88

Smart Growth Planning ...................................................... 96

Your "Freedom Tasks" for Big Results ........................... 106

You've Got This! Go Make it Happen! ............................. 114

Final Tip: The Golden Rule of Business ......................... 117

Are You Ready to Grow the Next Level? ........................ 123

About the Author ............................................................... 126

# Don't End Up in an Ambulance

**Scared, Dazed and Confused!**

What the heck had I done to myself? I was stuck in the back of an ambulance, and I'd put myself there. I'd been trying to grow my business, but instead, *I'd put myself in the back of an ambulance by doing it the wrong way!*

The goal of growing my business was admirable, it was good, and it was designed to help people. My wife was sobbing, and the ambulance officer staring at me kept saying, "You've had a stroke…blah, blah, blah …stroke …something, something… stroke." It was terrifying!

Now, I'd already known the pace I'd been running at in my business was clearly unwise. It wasn't sustainable and made no sense to anyone except me. I was working harder than ever and for less and less profit. The worst part was, I hadn't been aware of the consequences I would face if I didn't make some big changes. Suddenly, it was all catching up with me.

Scared, dazed and confused.

It was finally time to make some big changes.

Thinking back on it, when you fast forward to 12 months after the big ambulance experience I'd already transformed the way I run my business. My work life had drastically reduced to only 30 hours or so each week. I'd started working sustainably and was learning to "pace myself." I'd built a stack of new systems that got a lot more of my work done without my daily input.

Nobody has ever promised life as a business owner would be easy. I run two fast-growing businesses: Big Improvements Tutoring and About To Fly Consulting. Big Improvements Tutoring currently serves 600 families, offering tutoring services to low-ability students and making a real difference in their family. Given the small pond that I live in, it's a real success story.

My other business, About To Fly, is a business coaching and consultancy that's all about making business smoother and more profitable for owners who want to thrive in business without sacrificing their family life or personal life.

What you are about to learn isn't a bunch of untested ideas from a textbook. Instead, I will show you what I've learned in the real world of business so that you, too, can use the same strategies that have already made a massive difference in my businesses. I don't want you to go through what I went through on your way to growing a business.

Today, things have really turned around for me. I'm working only about 30 hours a week, playing plenty of sports, and taking my wife out for a date night every week. Life is a lot easier, but it's come from re-imagining and restructuring the way I work. My goal is to pass that knowledge on to you and help you grow your $1 million revenue business into a $2 million revenue business *without* having to sit in the back of an ambulance.

**Let's get started!**

## Is Your Business Built For Growth?

It's time to tackle the elephant in the room.

In the next few years, your business will either grow, or it will stagnate and slowly die. Some owners believe their business can stay at its current level and still succeed in the long term. However, with the speed of technological change and today's levels of systematic disruption in the business world, that is no longer an option.

I hate to be the one to burst people's bubbles, but you need to know this now, or you'll find out the hard way. Your business will either grow, or it will die. Your business can't stay like it is and still survive. If reading that causes you to feel annoyed or offended, then please put this book down now because you are not the sort of person who will get value from it.

Many business owners can't see the amazing opportunities waiting for them because they are so focused on running their business day-to-day that they haven't taken the time to deliberately choose a strategy for growth. Also, most owners initially succeed because of their excellent technical skills and passion for their craft, but unfortunately, that will only take your business so far.

A lack of vision, planning, guts, or creativity can all be barriers to your growth. Also, an acceptance of the status quo will keep your business at its current level and put a ceiling on your business' future. But this book was written to help you find and capitalise on the hidden gems of strength in your own business that are just waiting to be discovered.

This book is aimed at business owners who have been running their current business for a few years, who now have a stable, reasonably healthy business but want to grow it faster. If you're willing to put in the hard yards to make significant, profitable changes, then you've got the right book. Also, if you've got the courage to look your staff and key customers in the eyes and explain that there are better ways to run things so that everyone can benefit in the long term, then you'll be able to make great use of the strategies you're about to discover.

However, if the idea of growing your business scares you more than it excites you, or if you lack the personal confidence to make decisive changes in your business, you really need to put this book down and go back to the grind you're familiar with. That's because effective business growth requires boldness, hard work, and setting actions in motion. Growth happens when business owners try out new ideas by carefully calculating the odds, and then giving new ideas and systems a chance to work. You don't need to be reckless, but change always comes with some risk, and some people just don't have the stomach for that and aren't built for running a growing business.

To the best of my knowledge, nobody has ever written a book called "Safety First: How to Take No Risks, Overlook All Opportunities and Bury Your Head in the Sand While Your Business Stagnates". Although that may be a popular approach to running things, it's not a recipe for success.

Together, let's look at what it will take to significantly grow your revenue, and most importantly, to double your profitability. With the right strategies in place, you should be able to transform your business within just two years. If you're willing to give it a shot, then let's examine some strategies where it matters the most - your profitability.

## Keeping Profitability High

**Profit is Everything**

Let's start with the basics. "Profit" is not a dirty word. Profit is the oxygen for any sustainable business, and it's nothing to be ashamed of. At Big Improvements Tutoring, I serve children and their parents well and make a massive difference in their lives.

I'm not embarrassed to be well paid for it. I'm putting my own time and energy, as well as the happiness of my wife and kids on the line *every time I go to work.*

**New Growth Comes With New Strategies**

If you're reading this because you want to grow your $1 million business to a $2 million business, you need to know this: the growth strategies that got you this far will not get you to where you want to go.

Why not? It's because the skills you've mastered, the strategies you have in place, and the systems that are currently running won't get you to the next level of profitability. They're doing the job for now, but they're not enough to make the leap. You will need to make difficult and sometimes painful decisions to grow your business profitability while you grow.

## As You Grow, Your Prices Must Increase

Let's start by looking at your pricing. Your profitability will rise when you increase your prices as long as you're not alienating a large proportion of your clients or customers while you do it. I've never wanted to raise my prices, but I've had to because as your business grows, so do your costs.

You may assume it should work the opposite way - that as you scale, your costs should drop. The truth is that some costs do drop, but others go way up. As you grow, you will need new systems and more staff to run them. You're going to need to raise your prices to pay for these changes because otherwise your business will plateau at a certain size and face the unscalable wall of not having the money to build for growth.

Maintaining healthy profitability during growth periods requires you to be acutely aware of your key metrics and figures. You can't just hope the financial figures will work themselves out. I did that in my early years and got by, never being aware of how much profit I was making or not making. I just figured my business must be making a fair bit of profit because otherwise there wouldn't have been money in the bank. As you grow larger, that approach stops being feasible. Every step of the way, you must accurately know your revenue and profitability figures because if you don't, then you only need to make some minor mistakes to find yourself in surprisingly deep financial trouble. Have you realised you're not playing in the "little leagues" anymore?

**Keep your eyes on your key profitability scorecard.**

Consider what the key profitability metrics are for your business. In my tutoring business, I'm regularly looking at:

- how many customers we're serving each week;
- how many customers we gained this week;
- how many customers we lost this week;
- what the profit is per customer;
- what our overhead costs are;
- how much our overhead costs are cutting into our profits.

In the past I failed to take the time to measure these profitability factors, but I now measure almost everything. I would much rather have too much data instead of not enough.

## The Five Big Profitability Levers

You have five effective levers to increase profitability, so start putting them to use. They are:
1. increase your number of leads;
2. increase your conversion rate;
3. increase the frequency of customer purchases;
4. increase your prices;
5. reduce your costs.

**Increase Your Number of Leads**

A "lead" is a potential, future customer who is making an enquiry and deciding whether or not they should buy from you.

So, one way to quickly increase your business is to get a lot more new leads enquiring with you. You can grow that by putting more time, energy, money and marketing towards generating new leads.

Running special promotions at key times of the year can also give you plenty of new leads, but ensure that your promotion doesn't have a price discount because that reduces the perceived "specialness" of what you offer in the eyes of new clients.

Having a terrific website put together by an expert and making sure it is designed in a very Google-friendly way can also have a big impact on increasing the number of leads coming to you. Money spent on a well-built, carefully-targeted website is always a great investment.

Get the message out there, telling people who you are, how you can meet the needs of your target audience and why they should choose you. Speak more loudly and more clearly to the right audience to increase your leads.

## Increase Your Conversion Rate

A conversion is when you turn a lead (an interested, potential customer) into a paying customer. The number of conversions you have divided by the number of leads you started with (and turned into a percentage) gives you your conversion rate:

*Conversion Rate = Conversions ÷ by Leads x 100%*

There are many ways to increase the conversion rates of your leads. Ensure the right people hear about you, so you know you're marketing to people who already have a painful unmet need and already view you as a potential solution. Then, find easier, more effective ways for your potential new customers to learn about what you offer and come to a decision about whether or not to use you. Also, by giving your sales team better tools and better skills in how to persuade the "fence-sitters" to buy from you, your conversion rate will increase.

**Increase the Frequency of Customer Purchases**

Once you have a long-term customer, you can measure the frequency with which they purchase products or services from you, and how much profit margin is in each customer transaction.

By increasing how often your customer buys from you, you can significantly grow the lifetime value of that customer to your business. If you can find a way to set up a regular schedule of transactions, such as a monthly subscription or a "friendly reminder phone call" when those customers are likely to need a re-stock of your product, you can increase the number of purchases that customer makes from you.

**Increase Your Prices Every Year**

You can increase the profit margin per transaction by increasing your prices. This means as long as you don't lose too many of your customers by increasing your prices, every new sale becomes more profitable.

Most business owners fear increasing their prices because they believe heaps of their customers will leave them. However, as long as you are only increasing your prices by a small amount, most customers really don't mind. In my businesses, I implement a small price rise each year because people are happier to accept a small annual price rise than they are to experience a larger price rise implemented less often.

Most business owners believe that if you had half as many customers but double the revenue per customer, your profit will just stay the same. That's not true.

Here's the good news. If you lost half your customers, but doubled the revenue of the half that you kept, your profits would skyrocket. That's because you would only be serving half as many people, and delivering half as much of your product or service. Therefore, your overheads would drop enormously.

Clearly, it's not practical or realistic to suddenly double your prices, but this is how the maths behind it works and why price increases can be so helpful for profitability. I remind myself of this each time I fear losing customers when I increase my prices.

If you have niched your business fairly well, you should be able to increase your prices without losing many of your customers.

**Reduce Your Costs**

Cutting your costs is just part of the process of staying profitable. Just like weeds growing in a garden, so will your overhead costs gradually creep up on you unless you make the conscious effort to keep "weeding" them out. In our tutoring business, we've made some really tough decisions to adhere to this principle but the short-term pain was worth it.

We closed down two non-profitable venues so that the other nine locations could stay healthy. We changed the way our customers pay us. We used to manually invoice customers, but now we have them on a fortnightly direct debit system that is not only a lot more streamlined, but it's also reduced the amount of staff time and money we spend chasing overdue payments. We have also invested in a whole lot of new software to help our office staff get through their daily work tasks more efficiently, giving them more time to focus on customer service.

**Enjoy Making Profits**

"Profitability" is not a dirty word. Profitability is a must-have, a non-negotiable. I can't live without oxygen; your business can't live without a healthy profitability. You're going to need to laser-focus on profitability if you want to stay financially healthy while you grow your business to $2 million in annual revenue. Scaling on its own won't increase profitability, but scaling with the strategic use of these five levers puts you on the path to making real profits.

# Marketing Magic For Real Growth

**Three Questions for Effective Marketing**

To the uninitiated, marketing can look like hocus-pocus magic that only a marketing wizard can master. However, effective marketing becomes much easier once you can articulate the answers to these three questions:

1. Who are the potential customers with specific unmet needs who are willing to pay for your help to satisfy those needs?
2. What measurable results do you give your customers?
3. What are the particular ways or methods that you can meet people's needs better than your current options?

Once you know the answers to these questions and can articulate them; the next step is to find a way to deliver that message to your target audience.

**"Market Yourself," but Don't Do Your Marketing Yourself**

Do not do your own marketing. Your business has grown beyond that. You are no longer an independent, little operator anymore. Marketing is too important to keep doing at an amateur level once you reach the $1 million revenue mark. The good news is that a talented marketer can pay for themselves many times over, so it's actually more profitable to give the marketing role to someone else, plus, it saves you a whole heap of time to put into other things. Find someone exceptional and get their help to get your marketing message out to your future customers.

It's impossible to underestimate the importance of great marketing in your business growth strategy. When a business has a terrific, profitable business model, there is every chance it will succeed in the long run. Terrific marketing is the "not-so-secret ingredient" that can take a terrific business and launch it way, way further than its competitors who have merely average or above-average marketing.

In the earlier stages of your business, you probably grew a lot based on word-of-mouth referrals or simple, cheap marketing strategies. Now that you have grown, you are competing against larger, well-funded, strategically-strong competitors. Therefore your marketing needs to be excellent because what got you to your current size will not keep you there.

## One Dollar of Marketing Should Yield Two Dollars of Profit

Your business must discover a way to successfully deliver a message to your target market that you can solve their problems, meet their needs or make them feel happier. Often, successful businesses fail to invest the necessary money to have great marketing with an effective reach to their target audience. Often their owners are too short-sighted to part with the "seed money" to plant fantastic marketing and advertising in the short-term that will yield a harvest of new customers in the future.

Marketing takes a lot of trial and error. Expect to try quite a few strategies before you find one or two that work consistently well for you. Remember to test ideas and strategies with a small budget first to let your marketing prove itself. After these marketing plans have initially proven to be successful, you can then start to invest larger money behind those strategies.

With good marketing, you should be able to turn one dollar of marketing money into two dollars of profit later on. Once you have found effective ways to do this, invest heavily in it while it's working. Marketing techniques and campaigns only pay-off for a season, and then you will need a new strategy. That's because eventually your competitors will realise what you are doing and copy your marketing, or your marketing channel (newspaper, Google etc.) will gradually increase the cost of your marketing until it's less worthwhile for you.

Also, whatever you have been spending on marketing to get to $1 million in revenue, you will need to double to reach $2 million in revenue. Most people don't realise that until it is pointed out to them.

## "Awareness" is Not Worth Paying For

Measure whether or not what you spend on marketing comes back to you in profit. There are plenty of ways to do this. The easiest way is to ask new customers "How did you hear about us?"

Many inexperienced business owners continue to fund marketing methods that fail to generate increased sales and profits. They will delude themselves by saying, "It didn't make us a profit, but it did raise a lot of awareness for our business." You can't put "awareness" into your bank account. You can't pay your staff in "awareness." If "awareness" is all you've generated, it's time for a new marketing strategy.

## Carefully "Nichify" Your Business for Growth

To successfully grow your business, you need to offer customers something different than what the rest of the market sells. If you offer the same product in the same way your competitors do and use similar strategies your competitors are using, you can only get the results they will get. You may survive by playing the business game that way (although the odds are against you), but you can never thrive.

Instead, you need to have something "special"—something unique your business offers that makes you clearly stand out from most competitors. That's your 'niche', and it's your ticket to greatness.

If your niche is narrow enough, you won't have to work as hard to persuade customers to buy from you because you're not competing with everyone else.

Also, once you have found your niche, stick with it. You will have an easier work life because you can systematise things. After all, you will have been doing the same things for so long that you can do them with your eyes closed.

**Example—Tutoring Business Niche**

Let's take a real-life example of a business that I have grown from scratch by deliberately sticking to a carefully chosen niche - Big Improvements Tutoring. We serve over 600 current families in the super-competitive industry of tutoring.

Our Niche

We specialise in supporting children who are struggling with their schoolwork, by having them learn alongside only one other student and their tutor. We create hands-on learning tasks specifically tailored to the exact needs of each child, in a fun, energy-charged atmosphere.

Our Non-niched Competition

The rest of the tutoring industry puts children in groups of six or more and gives them worksheets or generic computer programs to follow. Our competitors can't give the same level of personal attention or create the nurturing, caring learning environment that we do. Also, the work that competitors give students in big groups can never be as carefully individualised as the work we give children because using our model, each tutor has only two students to focus on (not six or more). Also, competitors can't offer hands-on games and activities to help children learn because their "large groups with a tutor" model does not enable a tutor to facilitate this. The result of all these factors also means children enjoy receiving tutoring from us much more than they do when working with our competitors. Our niche lets us charge more and keep a happy, loyal customer base.

**The Five Commandments of 'Nichifying'**

Carefully Choose Your Niche

Choose one that is profitable, sustainable, and hard for others to compete with because it perfectly meets a particular type of customer's needs.

Stay Within Your Niche

You must stay within your niche at all times - refusing to be swayed back to the "mainstream" in your industry.

Price Your Niche

You must price your niche products or services at a premium, and at all times resist pressure to reduce your prices to non-niche prices.

Market Your Niche

You will market yourself boldly, clearly emphasising your "niche-ness" and refusing to be compared against standard products that are not as niche as you are.

Take Pride in Your Niche

You must always choose to be proud of your niche-ness and view your company as different from the rest of the pack - your staff and customers must be regularly reminded of the wonder of your niche-ness

**Niching Today Leads to Profiting Tomorrow**

Many business owners resist the call to "niche" because they fear it narrows the market of people they can sell to. Unless you are Amazon or Google, your business cannot serve an entire market. Instead, your goal should be to find a specific type of customer who has a slightly tricky requirement that most of your competitors would not find easy to cater for. Then, find a way to successfully meet those needs and charge a premium price to do so. Your particular type of customer becomes dependent on your business because others cannot serve them as effectively as you can. This is your businesses ticket to strong, reliable profitability into the future.

**Avoid Diversifying Outside Your Niche**

Many businesses want to diversify their income streams as they grow. Sometimes that is helpful, but often it is not. The danger is that while chasing the rainbow of diversification, businesses can be tempted out of their clearly defined niche.

As soon as you leave your niche, you leave the areas of strength your business is built on and renowned for. If you've got a winning recipe, scale that recipe and don't add new things to it!

I have rarely seen a business diversify profitably. Luckily, most businesses attempting to diversify don't succeed, so they end up getting rid of the diversifying-induced add-on extras once they have proven to be unprofitable.

In the worst cases I've seen, successful businesses have purchased another business that was viewed as complementary and then tried to integrate the new business into its existing structure. That is a recipe for disaster unless you are both in exactly the same niche, which is pretty unlikely.

Most businesses try to scale by broadening their offering, but instead, they end up wandering out of their niche. They'll find their profit margins dropping because what they offer is not much better than what competitors offer. Also because they are no longer niched as experts at everything they do, they need to develop a wider base of generalised skills to cater for a larger range of customer needs, so their workload and overhead costs increase substantially.

If you start up a new product line outside your established niche, you will need to build all the systems that go with it. You don't need that hassle.

There is a better way.

You are much better off putting your time and energy into scaling what you're already good at, so avoid the temptation to diversify or to step out of your niche.

## Hit the Right Level of Quality

Ready to bust some myths? A lot of people guess that making it from the $1 million turnover point to the $2 million turnover point is all about continually increasing the quality of your product. That's only half-true. Instead, the quality of your product needs to be at a high level but not an excessive level.

What does that look like in practice? Well, if I take my car for a car wash, I need it washed well. I'm not asking for it to be perfectly spotless. I'd rather pay a high amount for a great job than pay an exorbitant amount for a perfect job. It's the same with your business. As we're striving for more and more sales, we are tempted to keep pushing up the quality of our product and keep increasing service standards to maximise customer satisfaction.

I'm not saying you shouldn't have high standards for customer service and experience. However, what occurs when your standard is *excessively high* is that your costs skyrocket and then your profitability will plummet.

So, how do you know your customer satisfaction level is at the right level? Personally, I want my customers to receive a 92% level-of-quality experience. I always think 92% is just right.

I don't want to be delivering a 99% product because that extra 7% isn't changing anyone's life. It just increases the delivery cost.

On the other hand, I don't want to be delivering below 92%, because we are delivering a niche product, not an average product, so we need to back that up with solid quality to match our above-market price-point.

**Know how Customers View You**

Ask the Right Questions

In my business, a lot of my focus has been making sure I know the state of our customer satisfaction. I chat with a lot of clients and staff because I'm committed to understanding what our market wants from us.

I ask a lot of questions, like:
- What would you like to see done differently?
- What do you love now?
- What would you like to see remain the same forever?
- How did you hear about us?
- Why did you choose us?
- Are we communicating effectively with you?

By proactively creating these conversations, I get a reliable sense of how we're being perceived, and what people really want from us.

Ask the Right People

As a business owner, you're already aware of how important it is to be talking with your customers, but it is just as important to be chatting with your frontline staff who deal with clients each day. They are such a valuable source of information because they understand what upsets and what delights your customers.

To get brutally honest feedback from staff, owners need to create a healthy relationship with their frontline staff so their teams feel safe and confident to bring ideas and criticisms to the people who make the long-term decisions.

Really listen to them and act on what they tell you. You don't have to implement every suggestion staff have, but they need to know that you are willing to take on board what they're saying.

It's one thing to know how your long-term clients view you and it is highly likely you already have your finger on the pulse there. However, it's also vital to understand how initial conversations with potential clients manifest themselves. Regular conversations with frontline staff give you insights into the effectiveness of your positioning and your marketing strategy so you can be improving 'as you go'. You need to know about any problems early and deal with them decisively because having ineffective marketing will kill your business, and your frontline staff are your 'canary in the coal mine'.

A lot of business owners delude themselves into thinking they're in touch with what's going on, with how their business is being perceived. Unless you set up systematised, regular feedback processes, you will struggle to know when satisfaction levels are dropping or when there are negative trends developing.

Are You Fulfilling the Promises You Make?

Your business should always be creating a big promise to customers and delivering on those promises.

In our tutoring business, the unwritten, but assumed promises are:

- Your child will improve their skills.
- Your child will feel more confident.
- Your child will enjoy school more.

For our consulting business, About To Fly, the guaranteed promises are:

- We will give you significantly more in profits than what we charge you.
- You will get insightful, relevant, practical steps to improve your profitability.
- We have the skills and experience to really help you, because we only work with clients who have needs within the niche of our skillset.

Whatever *your* business' promises are, you have to be delivering on them. The first moment your promise falls short, your products or services cease being a high-quality, well-niched experience. You fall to the point of being a commodity just like everyone else. If that happens, it's a long journey back up to the top, so an ounce of prevention is better than a pound of cure.

**A Personal Note from Michael (the Author):**

By the way, if you're finding this book helpful, feel free to get in touch and ask for some free resources I can send you to help you grow your business.

That's because I love to help business owners get the best profits and lifestyle from their businesses.

Find me here:

www.abouttofly.com.

# Systematise Everything

**Improving Systems is a "Today" Job**

Let's have a look at the systems you'll need for moving from $1 million to $2 million in revenue. But first, let's give credit where it is due. I know for a fact you didn't get to $1 million without having some good systems in place. Unfortunately, the same systems that took you to $1 million won't get you to $2 million. That's why you need to examine the systems you've got and improve them, tweaking some things a little, changing other things a lot and completely rebuilding how you deliver in quite a few parts of your business.

It can sometimes feel daunting to discover you have to rebuild some systems from scratch. The good news, though, is once you upgrade your old, clunky systems into newer ones, they will match your current business needs (instead of the business needs you had when you were half the size you are now).

## A Journey of 1,000 Miles Starts Here

I want to encourage you with some practical examples of things you can do to successfully build your business on well thought out procedures and effective systems. That way, your business can operate with less reliance on you. Ideally, you should become unnecessary for day-to-day operations so you can focus on strategic matters that have more influence on profitability.

You've already read about my crazy experience of lying in the back of an ambulance with a suspected stroke. How did I get there? I got there by not having systems in place working for me. Instead, I was the system – like a human robot or a slave to my business. If you're in that spot, the great news is that you have the power to turn that situation around.

A few years have passed since then, and I've minimised most of my business' dependence on me. I can leave for a couple of weeks at a time, completely at ease that things will function successfully without me. A few years ago, I simply couldn't imagine leaving my business to operate without me for a few days at a time. What changed?

A lot of our processes changed. Here are some of the key steps that we took to systematise our tutoring business, and I hope these can help inspire you to set up more effective processes within your business.

Train Staff More Effectively

The way we train our staff has changed. Instead of just one-on-one training sessions, we incorporated video training and other automated online assessments of staff skills. It's now so streamlined that we only need one staff member to handle the training of 125 staff. This training system took eight weeks to build, but now only takes five hours each week to keep in motion for our entire workforce.

Scripts Save Time and Energy

Our customer phone calls are now all scripted. It doesn't mean that every conversation is scripted down to the word, but it does mean our frontline staff know all our policies and the points we want to get across in each customer interaction. It also means our office team can be quickly trained, and they can make the necessary decisions on the phone instead of needing to seek permission from more senior staff. You don't need to ask when you've already been trained in what the answers and solutions are.

Upgrade Your Email Systems

We have really changed the way we deal with emails too. We started using a product called Zendesk, which is a ticketing system for managing and tracking your customer and staff emails. That means you can't really lose sight of your emails because it helps you categorise them and track what has and hasn't been solved for customers.

The benefit of an advanced emailing system like *Zendesk* is that it simplifies email processes by giving us the opportunity to use pre-written, automatically filled in templates for many of our emails. For example, if a customer emails to tell us their child is sick or they need a catch-up session, then with a few mouse clicks we can get the right template, tweak some tiny details within the template and press 'send'.

The email magically goes out with the parent's name, child's name and most of the other details automatically entered by the system, so we often only need to tweak one sentence. So, by using *Zendesk*, we have turned a 5-minute emailing task into a 30-second task.

This is just one of many examples, and I'm not suggesting you need *Zendesk* in particular, because maybe there's another program that will be more suited to your needs.

Even a small business that doesn't upgrade to a better email system would at least benefit from turning most of its frequent emails into templates. I would estimate that less than 25% of businesses at the $1 million annual revenue size have a comprehensive series of templated email responses for their customers' predictable questions. The amount of time administrative staff spend on "re-inventing the wheel" with customer communications is so destructive to profitability.

If you keep your current email systems without improving them, your profitability will drop terribly because you will lose so much money on staff salaries. Also, you risk those staff eventually leaving you because nobody wants to do brain-dead administration tasks like we used to have to do.

If I was to share just one suggestion about upgrading an email system, it would be, 'Upgrade now'. One of the businesses I've done consulting for within About To Fly has over 3000 customers it needs to communicate regularly with. When I first started consulting for them, they were using *Microsoft Outlook* for their emails. Can you imagine how difficult it would be to track 3000 customers and all their communication using an email system like *Outlook* that is designed for an individual's personal computer? The best time to upgrade your email system is sooner than later.

Software is Your New Best Friend

Moving to the $2 million in annual revenue mark will likely mean using more technology to get things done instead of staff time. In my businesses, if I look at how we deal with our text messages, emails and at our client relationship management software, we have acquired new and better software at every step of the way.

We had to upgrade because the alternative to using great software would be a lot of chaos, drama and high overhead costs from all the unnecessary complaints we would be allocating our time to resolve.

Create Win-Win Policies

Our policies are clearer, cover more situations and are more systematised now than they were back when we were doing just $1 million each year.

When you're at that smaller scale, you can give a lot of exceptions and grace to people, especially those with whom you've built a long-term relationship. However, when you're growing to the next level, policies become essential.

For example, as the business owner, you may have a relationship and a "good level of understanding" with one of your long-term clients, but the other four staff members on the project don't know the client as well as you do. Your staff doesn't have a crystal ball to decide what interactions and decisions are right for a client if someone else has set up the relationship and the ground rules. Instead, they need to have clear, enforceable policies so customers know what to expect and your staff can deliver the consistent, appropriate level of service and deal with exceptional circumstances that inevitably happen. Wherever there are potential "grey areas" for customer expectations, great policies simplify life for everyone. That's why consistently delivered policies are an important part of scaling.

Handle Complaints Well

How you deal with complaints and misunderstandings needs to become systematised. When a business is small, the owner jumps on the phone and deals with a complaint whenever it pops up. It's usually a straightforward matter of finding out what the underlying issue is, creatively suggesting a solution that the client will be happy with and then making it happen for them.

However, the larger your business grows, the more other staff are involved in dealing with complaints and resolving them, which means you will need systems and processes in place for complaints.

I still occasionally deal with high-level complaints that come through our business when other senior staff are away, but I never deal with low-level complaints anymore. If a complaint is an unusual, significant issue, my staff knows they can chat with me for my suggestions, but then it's their job to solve things in line with our policies. For any complaint that comes to my desk, I want to understand where our system broke down and how it happened. I need to know this so we can tweak our system and avoid the situation repeating itself in the future. As a business grows, the owner's involvement with complaints and misunderstandings needs to become less focused on a particular customer, and more focused on building more effective systems, processes and policies that prevent future issues.

Dealing with Customer Payments and Overdues

Another system that needs to grow as your business does is in handling incoming payments and overdues. It's important to understand that the payment systems that served you when you were small become time-consuming, unreliable and inadequate as you grow. The more your business scales, the less of a personal relationship you have with your customers. That means there is less of a relationship-based sense of accountability and obligation felt by the client who owes you money, so that's where your systems come in and do the heavy lifting for you.

When we were a $1 million turnover business, we could just invoice clients, and most of them were fairly reliable. We could deal with payment problems individually, but now that we're dealing with 600 clients, we can't just send an invoice and hope they remember to pay. Imagine how much time and energy my team and I would spend chasing and dealing with overdue payments in that way!

These days, we've set up our customers on an automated direct debit system. When a new customer starts with us, they give us their credit card details so we can charge their account. It's turned our payment systems into a fortnightly payment routine, so it's just like a gym membership. Payments just keep rolling off customer credit cards each fortnight, and the only reason we would need to contact them about payments is if the usual process for charging their credit card is rejected due to lack of funds or other customer issues.

Also, as you grow, you will need to stop being gracious and lenient with customers who are struggling to pay their bills. If they can't afford your service, then they need to go and find someone else who is cheaper. Larger businesses simply cannot waste their office team's time on micromanaging unreliable payers, when instead they should be delivering great customer service to the 95% of people who want to pay reliably.

**Great Systems are Cheaper than Inefficient Systems**

When I advise business owners about steps and strategies for getting systems in their business set up more efficiently, one of the biggest roadblocks they see is the financial investment. Often, business owners believe they are too "poor" to spend money on software, but that is such short-sighted thinking. After all, every non-automated process you have in your business and every non-systematised procedure that requires extra staff time is increasing your wages bill. We've got several pieces of software that cost between $7000 and $12000 each year, and every one of them saves us more money in staff time than the software subscription costs. Sometimes business owners need to realise that great systems are worth setting up because they are cheaper in the long-term than running inefficient processes and systems.

Train Senior Staff to Build their Own Systems

It's been a challenge for me to give responsibility and authority to my higher staff members so they can change our policies and implement new, better systems. However, it had to happen at some point, otherwise, I would still be tied to my business, and it's clear that in the last six months I've become less and less involved in setting up new systems. Obviously, I've carefully chosen and carefully trained the right people for the "improve our systems" role, because the task is so important. However, it's something you must eventually hand over to your staff so you can break free from the "grindy" parts of building systems in your business. Instead, you can reduce your involvement (and time commitment) to become someone who is simply approving or tweaking the ideas that others see the need for.

Three Big Reasons to Get Your Systems Functioning Beautifully

Business owners have a tendency to micromanage their own businesses because they are good at their work. However, there are three main reasons why you need to let your systems work for you:

1. You will never sell your business for the price it is worth if a potential owner sees you as vital to your business' success. Instead, you need to be able to demonstrate that your involvement is an optional extra (like leather seating in a car). Well-built systems add enormous value to your business when you sell.
2. Most business owners are tied to their business, so they can't go away on holidays for a couple of weeks, and they can't spend time with their family on the weekend with their phone switched off. That's not a healthy way to live, and it doesn't allow the freedom that owning a business is supposed to give. Systems and procedures replace the need for the owner to micromanage issues that pop up.
3. When business owners can take their eyes off the day-to-day operations of their business, they can instead focus their attention on the high-level strategic things in their business that make a much bigger

difference to profitability. Every hour a business owner spends doing routine tasks within their business is an hour they are not spending working on business strategy and profitability. Business owners who are less involved in the nitty-gritty work have the time to build much healthier companies.

## Outsource like a Master

**Can You Afford to Outsource?**

To grow your $1 million turnover business to a $2 million turnover business, you're going to need to outsource more tasks than ever before. At the early stages of business growth, you didn't have enough spare money to pay contractors. Early on, your money was more valuable than your time. In the early days, your team had to do so many different tasks yourselves because you didn't have the budget to give tasks to others. Your money was more valuable than your time.

Just in case you haven't noticed, times have changed for you. Has your mindset changed to reflect your new circumstances? Many business owners are so focused on keeping costs low that they find themselves and their staff doing all sorts of mind-numbing tasks and consequently, they don't have time to focus on growing their business.

Now, at your stage of growth, it's time to understand that your time is far more valuable than money. You have a stable business so you know you have revenue steadily flowing into your bank account and you can rely on future revenue. So invest some of that into outsourcing some of your mundane work, allowing you to focus on the growth areas of your business.

**Outsourcing Gives Your Team Freedom**

It's important to find ways to get routine tasks off your own plate and paying others to do them is fine.

You simply can't scale without getting good at carving out sizable chunks of your team's workload, making other people or companies responsible for those tasks, and then holding them to account for getting those tasks done smoothly.

In my businesses, I work with literally dozens of contractors, a year, and in doing that, I've been able to ensure our core staff aren't dealing with a thousand little peripheral tasks anymore.

This means they can focus on what matters, on the things that only our team of "insiders" can deliver, like making sure our marketing is healthy and our customer service team are delighting our clients. Our team would not be able to focus on those important priorities if they had to get through the huge stack of routine daily tasks that we have given to contractors.

Now, back when we were a $1 million business, guess who did the office cleaning? We did. It needed to be done, and we did it. Do you think we do our own cleaning, now? Heck no! Obviously not!

Outsourcing Lets Your Staff Focus and Specialise

At our size now, if I assign one of our staff to do the cleaning, I'm inadvertently communicating the message to my team that, "I don't care about equipping each member of our team to thrive by specialising in different roles. I'm just making us all become generalists again!" As you scale, everyone has to become more and more specialised. Outsourcing creates space and freedom for your team to do that.

So, just examining our office cleaning tasks as an example, if we do those things in-house, I'm giving my team a job they probably don't want to do, and I'm using my talented, experienced staff to do a non-specialised and inexpensive task that I can get done by someone less-skilled. So outsourcing our cleaning to a contractor is not a sign of laziness at all. It's an important part of keeping our team on the tasks that matter most and which bring in the most profits.

Outsourcing to Experts Gives Quality

Let's take another example - this book that you are reading. Do you think I ever intended to edit it myself? No. I'll pass it off to one of my contractors who does an amazing job. After all, he's probably edited a hundred books for people in the past. He knows exactly what I want, what I need, and he's got all the tools to get the job done at a super-high standard.

It's time to stop thinking like a start-up or a sole trader. The days of being a generalist in your business are over, because your business won't grow if you split your focus and attention into a dozen areas of your business.

Get Rid of Book-keeping and Accounting

A vital thing to get out of your office is your book-keeping and accounting. At the $1 million mark, you were doing your own book-keeping and trying to keep that accounting bill low at tax-time. However, as you scale, accounting becomes something that is no longer just to keep the tax office happy. Instead, it turns into a way of viewing where your profits are coming from and areas that need tweaking. With good accounting and financial data, you can make accurate, timely decisions that help you grow.

We're not doing our own book-keeping anymore. One of our smartest and time-saving things in our business has been taking all of our book-keeping, giving it to an expert and saying, "Right, you sort this out." It's been oh-so-liberating!

My wife and I used to do our own book-keeping when we were small, but it's tedious, a bit stressful and it creates unnecessary tension in our marriage. That's pretty sound reasoning to get it off our plate.

My wife and I now take a few minutes to look at the financial figures each week or so, in order to make sure nothing looks unusual or worrisome, but the day-to-day book-keeping is off our backs. We're no longer sending emails back and forth to each other saying, "Can you charge this cost to such and such an account?" We've grown past that point, there are more profitable things we should be doing with our time, and we wish we had done that sooner.

## Marketing is my Precious Baby, but I Refuse to Change the Nappies

Marketing is a slightly different story. It literally is the key to your business health down the track. It's hard to outsource your marketing to someone who doesn't understand your business as well as you do.

A business has two main functions: to market well and to deliver well. You need to make sure that with something as important as marketing, you're handing it over to someone talented, reliable and certain to do an outstanding job. If you're the business owner, you know the finely-tuned message that needs to go out to the world, and it's dangerous to give your vision to someone else and just tell them, "Make it happen!" It doesn't work like that.

Outsourcing your marketing is like handing your own baby to someone else to hold. How do you do it? *You do it by outsourcing the <u>delivery</u> of the message only.* You, the master storyteller, stay in control of the message content. Let your marketing contractor control the means of communication - Facebook, website, blog, Google ads or whatever gets your message out there in the world. The core of the message is your baby, but you can outsource the time-consuming, messy stuff, like changing nappies and feeding to a nanny (in this case, your marketing contractor).

To be honest with you, I struggled to release my tight micromanaging grip on our marketing because it's so important. I've had to choose to let go of the implementation of the marketing, but I'm still responsible for the core messaging, and I do meet with my marketing team weekly or fortnightly to give feedback and check it's running in a healthy way.

It was very difficult for me to entrust more and more of our marketing to others because a lot of our growth in the early days was built on the marketing I was responsible for.

However, I had to accept that what got us to the $1 million dollar mark was not what would take us to the $2 million mark.

Choose the Right Contractors

I'm sure you've heard some scary things about outsourcing. It sometimes gets a bad name from people who do a poor job of it. There are a lot of different things you need to factor in before you just hand something over to someone. First, make sure you have the right person with the right skills, and then give them a few test cases to make sure they demonstrate good quality, skills, communication and timeliness. Initially, give them small tasks to do to test whether or not you can trust them with more important tasks later.

**Outsource Cost-Effectively**

Ensure your price is right too. There comes a point where the price becomes excessive, and you are better off keeping the task for your internal team. Alternately, you can find a contractor who will work within your budget.

Always remember that your contractors need you more than you need them, so it's their job to price accordingly.

## Use Upwork or an Equivalent Outsourcing Platform

A lot of my clients who are business owners do their outsourcing through an online platform called *Upwork*. *Upwork* is a way of using contractors from all over the world. You log into *Upwork* online, post a job that you need done, and wait a few days while people apply for it (sometimes up to 30 people apply for your job). Then you go through their applications, throw out the 90% of applications that look dodgy and interview the potential winners by video conference. When you think you've found the right person for the job, you should give them a test case or two first to see how they perform and if you're happy with them, you can give them more and more work.

If you haven't outsourced using a platform like *Upwork* before, find someone else who has done a lot of outsourcing and ask them to put you in touch with their contractors. That way you are working with people who have already been road-tested by someone you trust.

It is beyond the scope of this book to cover the many intricate details of how you go about setting up the right outsourcing arrangements, but a quick Google search will get you pointed in the right directions.

## Some Tasks are Easy to Outsource

They should be handed over as soon as possible. If you haven't outsourced to *Upwork* (or equivalent) contractors before, start with easy, safe tasks such as your graphic design or awesome copywriting. Seriously, what possible risk could you be taking by getting your next business cards drawn up or pamphlets written by a contractor? As you build your skills and confidence, you will be able to outsource other tasks such as your website, advertising, software-customisation, bookkeeping, computer troubleshooting and hopefully many other tasks. Your outsourcing becomes just another system that you build within your business and doesn't even need to be run by you - it can be run by other members of your team.

Outsource Suitable Tasks to People in Safe Countries.

At the risk of pointing out something obvious, you need to engage your brain before you go outsourcing willy-nilly. For example, I'm bewildered at the stupidity of large corporations such as phone companies or insurance companies who outsource their customer service phone conversations to people in countries where English is a second language. By outsourcing a task that is as important as "dealing with irate customers" they might save a few dollars, but they alienate many of their customers who hate trying to explain things to somebody who just doesn't quite have the English skills to understand their issues.

In a similar way, it would be foolish to outsource your customer billing or credit card processing to a contractor who lives in Iraq, Congo or some other fraud hotspot.

Think about your tasks carefully, be cautious, and give sensible tasks to people living in stable countries.

Outsourcing done well is a fantastic way of getting work done in a fast-growing business.

**Your Outsourcing Style Evolves.**

Now, as you scale from a $1 million business to a $2 million business, the scale and scope of your outsourcing needs to increase. When I was a $1 million business, I was outsourcing to individual contractors.

Now that we're bigger, we can't rely on just one contractor in each outsourced part of my business. I need to have a team of contractors. So, I'm now often finding myself outsourcing to companies or agencies instead of just one person.

You become very attached to your contractors after you've worked with them for a long time, and they matter to you. However, there comes a time where you can no longer rely on just one person to deliver because if they get sick or go away on holidays, your business will suffer. You may even find yourself doing their tasks while they are away.

You are no longer at the scale where you can just take on their responsibilities for a few weeks while they're away. So, the further you are down the growth path, the more you should outsource to agencies instead of individuals.

Expect Hiccups…and Occasional Disasters

Life isn't perfect and sometimes you need to roll with the punches life gives you. There are plenty of things that can go wrong when you outsource.

I've been scammed for a few thousand dollars on *Upwork* when contractors cheated the system. Let's just say the "helpdesk" on the *Upwork* platform was less than helpful when I reached out for their help.

I've also wasted thousands of dollars by giving tricky technical work to contractors who really didn't have the skills. Sometimes I couldn't have possibly known until later in the project, but mostly I was just naïve and a bit too trusting.

It's important to remember that when you outsource work, the person who is truly affected by the quality of the delivered work is still you – the owner. Therefore, when you outsource, you are still bottom-line responsible for the result, and it's up to you to get it right.

Probably 90% of what I have spent on outsourced contractors has been money very well invested. The disappointing 10% is just something I'll have to view as a learning experience.

Overcoming Illogical "Herd" Thinking

I've been using contractors overseas for parts of my businesses. My favourite contractors have lived in South Africa, the Philippines, Britain and Bangladesh. Some people view outsourcing as improper or unpatriotic, but I just can't understand how they reach that viewpoint.

I don't feel like I should employ people just from my own country, because there are a lot of people here charging high prices to deliver the same quality product as someone overseas would give me more cheaply. With profitability being one of my goals, it wouldn't make sense to only outsource within my own country.

When someone tells you that outsourcing to contractors is too risky, too difficult, or too "whatever dangerous-sounding reason" they've got, just remember that your alternative is to use very expensive labour from your own country. That probably forces you to choose someone with fewer skills than your experienced overseas contractor could give you for the same price. Not ideal, right?

Another foolish line of reasoning I've heard is that 'Outsourcing to other countries hurts our economy'. Really? I'll bet your clothes are made in China and your computer was made somewhere in Asia. Outsourcing is not a moral issue, and you are not responsible for your nation's entire economy. In fact, I take a lot of pleasure from pumping money into developing economies by employing their terrific people to help in my business.

Outsourcing Fast-tracks Your Business Growth

I know plenty of businesses that grew to the $2 million mark without outsourcing, but I would bet that most of them could have done it a lot faster if they'd made use of the outsourcing options available to them. Despite the challenges involved, outsourcing gets your peripheral work tasks done by talented people at reasonable rates, so it's something well worth making use of as you grow.

# Winning Mindsets, Goal Setting, Balance and More

To scale your $1 million business to become a $2 million business, you need to re-examine, re-evaluate, and probably change a lot of your pre-existing processes.

Another part of it is your mindset. You could have a business running beautifully that you could quite happily step out of or, largely step out of, but you don't - because your own mindsets are holding you back!

I'm going to share some business growth mindsets with you. Some of them will work for you and some of them won't, but that's okay. I would suggest you get a business coach or at least some really talented mentors with whom you can discuss these sorts of ideas and ask questions about mindsets.

## Losing a Few Customers is the Cost of Letting Go

A mindset I had to come to terms with is the idea that *as I become less involved day-to-day, problems will happen, things will break, and customers will leave.* I've had to get comfortable with that and think, "If I can have my 30-hour work week at the cost of losing 5% of our clients who were connected to me instead of the business, it's a good trade-off." To be honest with you, I'd gladly trade 5% of our clients or 5% of our profitability for not having to be at work. When you accept that you will lose some customers, you cease to fear it.

**Your Business is Tough, not Flimsy**

A mindset I've had to let go of is thinking our business was something flimsy, like a paper boat that would sink after a couple of waves. I've had to believe my business is secure; that it's a strong fortress. The wind may come against it, the rain might shower down on it, but the rocky foundation it's built on will withstand the weather, and I don't need to stand at the gates, walking to and fro, worrying that it will all crumble to pieces. I know I can go on holidays and the fortress will stay solid. That mindset has helped me tremendously because it enables me to make bolder strategic decisions without second-guessing myself as often.

**Focus on the System, not the Individuals**

Another mindset I've come to accept as we scaled is that it's less about me working directly with the customers and more about me building systems that work with customers. I keep finding myself wanting to make exceptions for particular clients who have been with us since we were small, but as soon as I step on that path, I break all the policies and procedures I've worked so hard to build. *I'm here to build systems. The systems are driven by other staff members who interact with our customers.* Whenever I try to get involved at the customer level, I'm keeping myself away from the strategic issues that truly deserve my focus and which have a much greater impact on profitability.

**Customers Need a Consistent Experience**

I've had to wrap my mind around consistency. I tend to navigate towards doing complex things with all the tools I have at my disposal, but sometimes that's not the best idea. If I step out, and someone else steps in, they're not able to follow my processes, and they're going to deliver at a lower quality level than my own. So, I need to keep myself off the tools and stop trying to make everything perfect. I need to let other staff do a very good job instead of micromanaging by getting involved to ensure an excellent job. Why is that? It's because I need the *delivery to clients to be consistent, and by me stepping in with my super-specialised experience, the customer will be disappointed next time when a less skilled staff member is working with them.* I've done my craft for so long that my delivery is fantastic, but I don't want customers experiencing *fantastic* today merely to experience *very good* tomorrow because that inevitably creates *disappointment*. There are lots of times I've had to choose to NOT give customers above-and-beyond levels of service. That's because "above-and-beyond" paradoxically creates drama, because the next time they come to us, they're going to want the same unrealistic level of service again. It is healthier for the customer experience to be consistently *very good*.

**Be "Firm" not "Nice"**

Let's talk about the idea of being "nice" and what it costs you in business. I need to care about people, about customers and their experience, but I can't afford to make exceptions for people just because I'm "nice." Clear and consistent policies need to replace "nice" individual exceptions. "Nice" will get you to the $1 million mark. "I'm happy to work with him! He's such a nice guy!" At the scale you are at, it's not about you anymore; now it's about your business. You can't afford to be nice. Nice means, "Look, I will put own rights aside. I'll put whatever serves me aside, and I'll just wear the consequences on myself when I'm not taking responsibility for you." That's what nice means in business. You can't afford to have that mindset anymore. Your new explanation needs to be, "Yes, I've done that for you in the past, and I was happy to do that for you as a one-off. Unfortunately, I can't do that anymore, and our policies are really clear that we never needed to do that. We were going above and beyond when we did that for you." Be less nice, and instead focus on being consistently great within pre-defined policies that are fair to everyone (including yourself).

**Be Focused on the Group**

This one is key. Be secure about your business, rather than being worried about how you're perceived. Do you think big companies like Coca-Cola or Uber care what *you* personally think of them? No, they don't. They care about what the data tells them and how their *entire customer base* views them. You can't afford to be insecure. You can't afford to be worried, "Oh! What's that customer thinking of me? Were they happy with the work we did for them?" Now, I'm not suggesting you ignore customer feedback or customer experience, but I am suggesting that you can't base your decisions on the response of a couple of clients. Instead, focus on how the entire group of customers perceives you and if they feel they are getting what they need. Be secure about who you are as a company and what you offer.

**Reduce Customisation and "Special Requests"**

I've had to say to my staff, "This customer is overly-demanding, and if they don't like what we offer, they can choose to go somewhere else."

I used to be swayed by unreasonable requests saying to clients or customers, "Yes, here's what we do. Here's what you're asking. I think I can find some sort of middle ground." I don't do that anymore. Now I say to them, "Well, here's what we do, and here's what you're looking for. For that specific thing, I think you should consider our competitors. If, however, you want what we offer, here's why I think we would serve you quite well, but you can choose whatever works for you." Becoming secure in yourself means you're no longer chasing demanding customers. Instead, you're saying, "Here's what we can do for you. You know you don't have to take it. But if you do want this, we'll be 100% behind you. If not, that's okay." This approach stops you from being manipulated, the way you were back when you only had 20 customers. For $2 million, you need to put a stop to the individualisation of things.

**Overwork is unprofitable work**

I don't know many people who went into business because they genuinely wanted to work 60-hour work weeks. Yet, many of the business owners I work with find themselves trapped in weeks just like that. If you're in this situation, something needs to change. I believe that whatever hours you work beyond the 45 hours mark, probably aren't adding much value to your business anyway. Beyond 45 hours, your extra time produces tired, sloppy, uninspiring work and saps your long-term enthusiasm. Instead, build yourself a more relaxed balance of work-time and recharge-time. You can achieve that partly through building effective business systems and making sure your business is profitable. When you overwork yourself, you massively increase the risk of serious health problems, irreparable marriage issues, or just becoming a doom-and-gloom sad person. Do whatever it takes to get your work hours under control. Otherwise, there's no point in growing your business.

## Mindset is Less Profitable than Action

People cannot succeed in business without choosing mindsets that will work for them, but we need to base our mindset on what is real and true in our business. Base every decision on facts, not a blindly positive mindset. Yet the power of helpful, empowering mindsets that lead to productive prioritising and actions is very much underestimated among business owners.

## Rethinking Minimum Viable Product

Let's kill a sacred cow - even one that is a very helpful sacred cow. The infallibility of the "minimum viable product" approach to business growth.

The philosophy of minimum viable product is this: You do not need your product or service to be perfect before you sell it. Instead, you should create something that is "good enough" to sell, and then tweak your product while it is in the market, evolving it into a fantastic product in the long-term.

Let's be crystal clear: I am a massive fan of minimum viable product in business. I'm a devoted adherent to that style of doing business. I want to shoot super-straight on that. However, as you grow, you can't afford to keep playing minimum viable product as much as you used to.

Back when my team was a smaller business, we were running minimum viable product experiments regularly. We were always trialling new things, always tweaking, and it was great. You can get by with a certain level of quality when you are small enough to have personal relationships with each of your clients, but as you scale, the value of the minimum viable product technique becomes a bit trickier and riskier, in practice.

I'm not suggesting that you should steer away from the minimum viable product approach when implementing changes. It's just that it's now time to be a bit more measured and planned about it.

In the past, I might have run around 30 or 40 experiments a year to tweak things. We were experimenting with minimum viable product styles of small changes to how we delivered our service, partly to improve and partly to look for feedback from our customers on what they really wanted.

Nowadays, I'm doing less than half that number because the experiments themselves are bigger and the scale of energy and effort required to make new ideas work is bigger.

Another challenge we face is that our brand is built on consistency of experience so when customers experience an experiment, even when it appears to be successful, the inconsistency from your normal delivery does have a slightly negative impact on your reputation.

That's why, as you grow, your standard of "minimum" in minimum viable product thinking needs to be significantly higher than it used to be when you were smaller.

Also, we don't need to be running a million experiments all the time to gauge customer responses because we've now got years and years of accumulated knowledge from previous customer feedback.

So, we've reduced how much experimentation is happening in our business, because as you scale, you need to rethink how you implement the minimum viable product philosophy.

However, this must be kept in balance because it is profoundly dangerous to stop trialling new things. If we stop innovating and experimenting, then we'll go back to being unadventurous, boring, and risk-averse within a couple of years. In fact, we would end up stale and stagnant like many of our competitors, because that's what happens to larger companies in most industries after a while. So, do proceed with minimum viable product experiments but just be more measured and careful about it, because your customers expect consistency from you.

# How to Spend Your Work Time for Best Growth and Profitability

### Live by the 80/20 Rule (Pareto Principle)

The 80/20 Rule (also known as the Pareto Principle) is that 80% of your results come from 20% of your actions. This principle has been demonstrated to work most of the time in business, politics, agriculture, and pretty much whatever else you can think of. Now, it's up to you to make it work in your business.

I believe that most of your gains in profitability comes down to one thing - knowing how to use the Pareto principle to focus your time and energy in the 20% of tasks and projects that will have the biggest impact in your business.

Ask yourself daily, "What's the one action I can take that's going to have the biggest impact?" Once you know what that action or task is, make sure you do that as a much higher priority than the rest of your daily work.

The alternative is to get all details-focused and miss the main things. Our parents' generation used to say, "Worry about the cents and the dollars will look after themselves." What a myth! That is the opposite of living by the 80/20 rule, and that is NOT how you succeed in business in this day and age.

Instead, each day, pick the most important tasks you have control over, execute them well, and delegate, deprioritise or disregard everything else.

By starting with the 80/20 mindset, most business owners make great leaps forward in how they prioritise. Without it, you will feel torn in a dozen different directions, and the health of your business will be jeopardised.

**Delegate Wisely and Supportively**

Prioritise getting great processes and systems into your business because that's what is most effective for growth at this stage of the game. Discard whatever business routines or activities take your attention away from these things.

More of your time needs to go towards setting goals and criteria for your key staff and then supporting them on the journey when they have questions. Less of your time should now go towards micromanaging or working on their tasks with them. Instead, focus on clarifying goals and criteria and then let them do their tasks with more autonomy.

Remember that delegating is not the same as abdicating. Once you hand roles over, you still need to create systems so there are due dates and clear criteria for the completion of the tasks. Also, when tasks are not completed, together with staff members, you need to work out what went wrong, and what it would take to solve things for the future. Fix whatever system is holding people back from succeeding in their roles.

Most people view productivity as being all about making tasks efficient, but your goal now is to stop thinking about tasks and just focus on impact and prioritising goals for your staff, then supporting them to work with less dependence on you.

**Say "No" to More Requests**

It's time for you to say "no". You'll be saying "no" to a lot of tasks you used to do regularly in your business. You'll be saying "no" to many requests that you would have previously agreed to because you are now playing *a much bigger game* – building a long-lasting business. This will come as a surprise to your staff and customers who are used to you helping them in little ways, but you just don't have the time to do that anymore.

What actually happens when you keep meeting people's time-consuming requests is that you're taking your eyes off the systems you're supposed to be building and getting involved in your business in a hands-on and micromanaging way. How counter-productive!

As you start to say "no" more often, it's important to have an authentic expectations-setting chat with the people you are saying "no" to and explain why you've changed your approach. Let them know that you want to help and want them to succeed, but that your capacity for helping is reduced by the extra demands of growing your business.

Generally, they will not only understand, but proactively look for ways to minimise their requests of you.

Also, try to be diplomatic when you say "no" to people. A better phrase to use would be "I'd love to help, but I can't because I've got my eyes on some other projects right now and I'm a bit overloaded by them."

**Micromanaging is Your Kryptonite**

Just like Superman stays as far away from kryptonite as he can, I regularly remind myself that the micromanaging mindset is dangerous and will stop my business from getting to the next level.

The "sin" of micromanaging happens when you get very focused on the way a task is being done, and then you exert heaps of your influence on ensuring that task is done using your methods and to your standards. Micromanaging is appropriate in the early stages of training someone, but once they show some proficiency, it's important to step back a bit and reduce your level of oversight, feedback and control.

Micromanaging is devastating to the growth of your business because it keeps people dependent on you as the leader instead of effective at using well-designed systems to do their work.

Every business owner I know has a tendency to micromanage, and it's something I need to guard against. You probably don't even realise when you're micromanaging. In fact, most people think they don't micromanage at all! You can go to the most micromanaging micromanager on the planet and ask, "Do you micromanage?" He will shake his head and swear, "No, I don't."

You can't see micromanaging tendencies and habits in yourself. You might have to ask your staff, "What am I doing that I shouldn't be doing? What task could I outsource to others? What do you think I should do?" Get some feedback from them. They will probably give you a much more accurate reflection than your own perception.

It comes down to the strategy of what you're going to be involved with and what your tasks are within that bigger role. I don't want to be micro-producing every little thing, for example. I just want to have input on important things and into the strategy. I want to be guiding the team without actually "doing the doings." Most business owners who are working super-long hours each week are stuck doing that because they haven't understood this principle.

The captain of a submarine might say (using their own terminology of course), "All right, let's turn left by 15 degrees and go in that direction," but he's not the one at the actual steering wheel. He's just setting the direction. As the owner of your business, you need to be like that captain.

You probably wholeheartedly believe you're already doing "just fine" in this aspect of leadership. Almost every business owner genuinely believes that, but most aren't truly acting as the captains of their ship. Instead, they are still trying to be the navigator at the wheel.

## Drop Your Most Annoying Clients

Do you have particular customers who drive you crazy and who you wish you didn't have to work for? Well, what are you waiting for?

We've all got clients who we don't look forward to interacting with, so we need to ask ourselves why we are continuing to work for them. Are you so short of clients that you really need them? I don't think so. Let them go. Don't work for people who are unkind, unreasonable or overly-demanding.

Maybe it's time for some necessary, long-overdue conversations with these clients to reset their expectations of what you will and won't be prepared to deliver for them. If they understand the new boundaries and are happy to play by the rules, you've just turned a "nightmare client" into a 'manageable client'. However, if they don't like the new arrangement and choose to leave, you will save yourself a lot of headaches and stress.

Once you know that it is time for a client to go, do it gently, so they don't leave you a horrendous Google review or an equivalent form of revenge. Simply explain to them, "I understand what you need, but I also know that my team can't deliver that for you, so what I'm going to do is help you find someone who can give you what you need for the long term." Then, send them to one of your competitors who you think would be a better fit for them. Everybody wins and ends up happy.

Defend your staff from nasty clients by creating policies that enable your team to say "No" to them, or to turn them away. Your staff morale and their willingness to enthusiastically focus on more profitable areas of your business will both improve. You wouldn't let nasty people stay in your home, so don't let them stay in your business.

**Get Outside of Your Office**

Here's one of the secrets to being effective. *You need to work more outside of your workplace.* It's hard to get the important strategic things done when you're at the office with all the seemingly urgent and dramatic day-to-day events playing out in front of you. I spend most of my work-time working from home because I can focus. If I work from my workplace, too often I overhear customer issues or other dramas that drag my attention from my work. My team don't need me to solve these things for them, and it's counter-productive for me get involved. Instead, my job is to make sure our strategy is right, and I'm better off doing a lot of that from home. That way, as a leader, I can focus on ensuring we're going in the right direction rather than being distracted by every little event happening in the workplace.

**Spend Time Learning**

It's tempting to think that you don't need to continue learning because you have been so successful. In one sense, it is probably true that you don't need to continue learning about your craft or trade. In another sense though, more than ever before you need to learn how to build and steer your business and that has nothing to do with the skills most of your employees are using.

So, spend a lot of your time "up-skilling." Learn how to do the tasks that actually matter. Before you know it, maybe in a year or two, you might be running a $3 million business or a $4 million business. You have to be ready for that challenge when you get there. I spend at least 10% of my work-time up-skilling my personal business skill-set. I read at least one business book a week, plus I watch a lot of online video-training so that I'm really on the ball with the skills I'll need down the track. I didn't need these skills in the past, but I'm developing them now because they will pay off later.

So, if you're not yet spending at least 10% of your week growing and up-skilling, this may indicate you are still stuck in a "get tasks done" mindset, instead of a "build a business" mindset. You are one of your business' most important assets, so it's time to grow yourself. Start getting ready for the future by developing your skill-set now.

## Leading and Managing Staff

Let's examine what your staff need as your business grows because the systems and practices you used for leading a close team of staff when you were smaller won't allow you to expand in a healthy way.

At my stage of the game, I have 140 staff members plus some contractors who work for us. That's a lot of people. I can't manage 140 people, and I don't want to have a million managers of managers. I want to have systems managing people rather than people managing people. Without great staff management systems, your business will be a place of confusion, drama, inefficiency and inconsistency. Eventually, your staff costs will spiral out of control, and you will struggle to generate a profit. You'll become like a typical government department rather than a lean, efficient business.

**Value Staff Motivation**

At this stage of the game, your staff's motivation is less related to you and more related to the feeling of team success. It's about the mission they've all bought into.

They need to fully understand their purpose in the company and why they are employed, what their role is with the customer and what difference they're making in the world as a team. That's the motivation for them. It's no longer about caring to help the leader get to wherever he or she wants to go.

If you have effective systems and are managing people who have bought into what the company stands for, then keep reminding people why they're working for a business which is making a positive impact on the community. Trust me, you'll have a very harmonious, very healthy workplace.

There are over 100 different theories on motivating staff, but I believe it all boils down to this: people want to work in a friendly workplace where they are paid well, treated with courtesy and where their efforts are clearly and regularly appreciated. If you find ways to make that happen, you will always have motivated, effective staff. If you have a staff morale problem, it probably indicates you have missed the mark in one or a few of these areas.

**Help Staff Specialise in their Strongest Skills**

Your staffing at the $2 million annual revenue point is going to be very different from where you are at now. At the $1 million point, you have to employ a lot of "generalists"—people who have a reasonable level of knowledge in a wide variety of areas. For example, the staff member answering the phone is the same person processing various client requests and simultaneously dealing with client documentation. You can't keep doing that as you grow. Instead, you need more staff, and each staff member needs to specialise more in the key areas where they can have the most positive influence on your business.

I found this to be very difficult as our tutoring business was growing. Our administration and office staff were used to being generalists. It was the kind of environment where any one of us was able to jump in and do a task.

As we changed this, we had to regularly reassess and say, "Hold on, who's the best at this task? Give it to her." Certain people are better at dealing with complaints, so let them handle them. Other people are happy to do repetitive, procedural tasks, so funnel that type of work to those staff.

It's a real mind-shift because you spent years building up your staff into the generalist mindset of "Oh, we can all do everything!" Now you're going to have to change that and say, "You know what, that's how we used to do it in the past. Our new way of doing things is dividing the roles and specialising." We've had to be a lot clearer on what exactly each person's role is, what tasks they are responsible for, and what lies outside of that.

**Hold Staff Accountable for Results**

When you're running a small business, and you see staff giving 100% effort, you'll value and appreciate them, but find it hard to hold them accountable for results. However, now that you've grown, you need to help people become results-focused instead of efforts-focused. As you scale, success is less dependent on people's effort. Instead, success will come from choosing the right goals and then holding people accountable for achieving particular results that lead to those goals.

This doesn't mean you can afford to overlook or devalue people's efforts. Definitely, appreciate and praise your staff for efforts, but also be aware that success is not dependent on people's positive intentions anymore. At your new, larger scale it's about the results achieved.

## Build Strong Relationships with Your Management Team

Your relationship with your staff becomes less personal as you move from a $1 million turnover business to a $2 million turnover business. When we were still small, I was giving out movie tickets to our on-the-ground staff, buying them a coffee, or just doing whatever I could to convey, "Hey, I care about you as a person, and I'm here to support you in your work." However, at the size that we've grown to now, no matter how much I want to, I just can't do that.

Now, our systems (not me) reward staff and helps them feel valued. For example, around Christmas, all our staff get a set of movie tickets as a "thank you." It's not as personalised, but it's still a way of conveying that you value them. Key staff will receive other small, but heartfelt "thank you" bonuses from me, but I can no longer personalise these to 140 staff.

## Conduct Effective Staff Meetings

Staff meetings are another big process to improve as you grow. At $1 million, I could get by with intermittent staff meetings here and there. It was fine. I made sure the staff knew what had to be done, but I didn't need the same level of input from them as I do these days. We now have a fortnightly staff meeting with our key leaders. We discuss our current priorities, difficulties we are facing, and things that need to be worked on. It takes us about 90 minutes, and it sets us up for a great fortnight. We didn't need any of that before. When we were small, the planning and strategy was mostly stored in my head and diary. That was enough to get us by.

Of course, when we were smaller, there were things I needed to share with certain key staff members because I wanted their input and their insights, but as long as the main strategy was in my head, it would usually work.

However, at the scale we're at now, it doesn't work like that unless I become some sort of robot or suddenly decide I want to work a million hours a week (not likely!). We need those staff meetings with key staff.

Once a week, our other staff will get together in their teams to examine any issues they face. They'll raise problems and pass suggestions up the chain-of-command, saying, "Hey, are you guys aware that this is going on? What can we do to tweak this?" In the past, you may have survived without having these planned, formal meetings, but you can't anymore. You need to make them happen, but they need to have a purpose and good execution.

The key thing with each meeting is focusing on specific outcomes. Every meeting must end with each participant knowing what the next steps to take are. If they don't get to that point, the meeting was a poor use of time.

Also, at the management level, managers need to be aware of how we are going in relation to our key metrics such as sales figures, customer growth numbers and overhead costs. We call this our scorecard. If you don't have a scorecard, you need to get one otherwise your leaders will be making decisions based on emotions instead of facts and data.

Regular, well-planned, well-run meetings that lead to great decisions and measurable results are vital for your business as you grow. You can't continue living on the owner's talent or insights. It's not just the leader telling everyone what the plan is - it needs to be a team effort. That's because your business must be built on systems and teamwork, not on the owner.

# Mastering Company Culture and Health

## Success Comes from the Team, Not the Leader

What keeps your company on track when you're not there? What keeps everything on track when you're overseas for a month, and you're not involved? In the long-term, the health of your company is not actually built on the strength of your leadership. Instead, it comes down to the health of your company's culture.

Once your business grows past the $1 million mark, your ability to personally influence day-to-day outcomes diminishes. That's because your company's effectiveness cannot be based on your performance as a leader, but it actually becomes more about the culture that your team have built and the efficiency of the work practices the team uses.

If I think back to when we had only $1 million in annual business turnover, I didn't have to focus much on the health and culture of my office team. I was there every day directing staff. I could see potential problems from a mile away and prevent them from causing damage. We could deal with issues because I'd had so much experience and I was right there on the ground to make the necessary decisions.

We have since grown to twice the size we were, and I'm not even in the office for most of the time. I prefer to work from home so I'm not distracted by day-to-day office activities.

What keeps the team wholeheartedly pursuing their goals when their boss is not around?

Also, a firmly-embedded, vibrant culture releases you to pursue other things in life apart from your business.

How do your leaders know which opportunities to pursue and which are just distractions from your real purpose?

What ensures that the business continues to fulfil its goals and purposes without getting distracted?

The health of your company culture determines its effectiveness when you are out of the picture. So, how do you make sure that the culture you built as a team is healthy?

## Leaders Must Understand Your Niche

First of all, ensure the leaders within your business understand the importance of staying within your niche so they don't get distracted by other opportunities which could take your company off-course. As you already know, by remaining firmly in your niche, you're already stronger than many of your competitors, and that feeling of advantage brings in a sense of pride for your whole team.

## Your Company Lives or Dies by its Values and Purpose

There is a huge difference between having clearly-declared company values and purpose, and actually living them out. Almost every company declares that its values are "great service," "caring people," and "high commitment to quality," or something like that, but the reality is usually very different. Your company values and purpose are either lived out well in practice, or they are just meaningless words. Also, if the company values are not being lived out in reality, it is usually because the leader has not been consistent in living out those examples in the early years. That is both bad news and good news.

The bad news is that if you're not happy with your company's culture, it is largely a direct result of your own actions, choices and the example you have set over the previous years.

The good news is that you have the ability to influence your company values even if this has not previously been an area of strength for you.

In our tutoring business, every staff member is trained and reminded of our values and purpose. They are very aware that we are here to deliver a massive, positive change in every child's life, and we achieve that by providing life-changing tutoring.

Right from when we started, our clearly-stated focus has been, "We're here to change lives, and we're here to make a difference."

Anything that doesn't contribute to that really doesn't belong in our business and staff hold me accountable on that more than I hold them accountable.

**Reinforcing Company Values with Staff**

All staff members must understand and be able to articulate what your company's core values are.

Ideally, the values should be written on a wall somewhere. *Every single staff member* should be able to articulate your values and purpose. It does not matter whether each staff member is reciting verbatim what the values and purpose are, or just putting them into their own words. It just matters that all staff members can explain what your business stands for and is aiming for.

In our tutoring business, we have about four sets of hour-long training videos that staff members watch in the first six months of their work with us. We clearly state our values and purpose in each of those videos. We also have our values and reason for being here written on the office wall and on our website. Also, whenever we have staff training days, we ask the question "Are our core values and purpose being lived out in what we do on the ground?"

There are a variety of techniques for stating and reinforcing culture within your business. However your team chooses to do that, it's important that reinforcing culture is something that occurs regularly, systematically and matches reality.

Our staff feel proud because they all know we are succeeding in our values and purpose because it is measurable by the feedback we receive from our customers.

## Dealing with Threats to Company Health

The health of your company's culture can suffer when people become self-absorbed or play politics. In most workplaces, there will be regular, small issues that create conflict. When leaders see these issues playing out, it's important to deal with them decisively and fairly quickly.

At the scale you're at, you probably have about six or seven key staff, and their depth of relationship with you will usually be a bit more shallow than back in the days when you only had two or three key staff. It's important to resist the tendency to be passive or optimistic because when there are threats to staff morale or company health, they need to be noted and addressed. If the business owner or the key leaders fail to drive the company culture, then it will become driven by politics, which can really hurt a business.

## Only Employ People Who Enhance Your Culture

If you're interviewing someone who is conveying values in opposition to what your business stands for, you need to stop interviewing them and jump to the next candidate. When your team is hiring new staff, they need to look beyond the skill set of potential employees to also take into account whether or not the applicant will enhance your company's culture and enthusiastically live by the company's values.

If you accidentally hire someone who dislikes what your business stands for, they need to leave. They're not built for your team. When it comes to company health and company culture, you need the whole team to be positively contributing to the company's mission.

That's because the more that your business grows, the less direct influence you have on the company culture. Therefore, the team needs the right people to build and reinforce a culture that is enjoyable to work within, that you've all subscribed to, and that can succeed in the long-term.

**Your Employees Must Match Your Culture**

Also, if your current employees don't like what the company stands for, they really need to find somewhere else to work. That doesn't mean employees must agree with the owner's values, but they need to buy into the company's values and mission. When people don't fit into the culture, it isn't the company's responsibility to change, but instead, it is the employee's role to either live by the stated culture and values or find a different company with a culture they are better suited to.

**Face the Business Owner's Weaknesses**

Let's be straight here - I'm a business owner, and I've got weaknesses. Every person has their own struggles and weaknesses. There are things I sometimes do that make work feel unnecessarily difficult for my team. For example, I tend to try and create too many "minimum viable products" and experiments at once, and that creates work for others. I tend to go off on growth tangents too easily and sometimes run the risk of leaving staff feeling confused about current priorities. Sometimes my timing is not ideal for implementing new things because I have a tendency to be overly optimistic about what we can achieve in short timeframes. I also have a tendency to make snap decisions without thinking through all the steps to implement them.

I know my weaknesses, and my staff have permission to let me know when I'm doing things that are not helpful for them. By doing my best to be suitably humble and open to people's feedback, I semi-regularly receive discouraging feedback, but it sets the tone for the culture we have of being transparent and real. However, it is certainly worthwhile, because my commitment to my company's success and growth is greater than my need for approval or validation.

Most business owners are fearful of revealing their weaknesses to their staff, but usually, that's because they are living under the false belief that their staff are not already acutely aware of their weaknesses. For the sake of a healthy culture, it's important for an owner to be honest and transparent and to take people's feedback on board.

**Policies Give Stability**

"Policy" is not a dirty word. Having clearly defined, fair policies plays an important role in keeping company culture healthy. There is a real sense of certainty and freedom for your staff members when they have clarity about what they should say "Yes" and "No" to and this comes from the quality of your policies. Ideally, the goal is for each employee to be aware of all relevant policies in place for dealing with customers and other staff, and for each member of your business to feel confident that the policies are just and fair.

In our tutoring business, we created many of our policies with the help and input of our front-line team. Our goal was to create generous and fair policies, but also to do it in a way that ensures we won't be taken advantage of. Once you've got those policies, they become a healthy part of your culture. They prevent staff from needing to make hard decisions when people ask for exceptions to the rules. Your policies create a sense of confidence in your staff members because they know when to push back on customers and when to give ground.

It creates the freedom to have a confident, healthy company culture - saying "'Yes" to people when you can, "No" when it's necessary, and feeling secure about both.

**Celebrate Successes**

Find ways to celebrate when the team is successful. Every "win" needs a celebration, even if it's simply a verbal "thank you." Every time someone does something that's truly "above and beyond," people need to be personally recognised for it and thanked. I'm not suggesting you to give them a cake with their name written in chocolate every time they do something outstanding. Just notice their exceptional work and value it because they (like most of us), are human beings with feelings. The key reason they come to work is they feel like they have something to offer and believe others in the business will treat them accordingly. If you take that away from them by withholding credit for a good job, they're not going to be around next year.

**Being Real about Finances**

Be transparent about your business' performance. There is something our Big Improvements Tutoring does that most companies lack the courage to do, and I encourage you to consider it for your own business. In fact, many people would initially believe this practice to be a dangerous idea, but it's worked quite well for us, so I'm going to be open with you and share.

We choose to be financially transparent with all our key staff and medium-level employees about our figures, our profit margins, and our future plans and strategy.

Who gets to see all these figures and plans? Well, if you look at the structure of our tutoring business, you'll see there are four of us at the top level of management. In the next layer down our administration team is comprised of six people who are our visible frontline team. The layer below that is made up of a hundred or so tutors who deliver the actual tutoring.

I want our 4 key top-level leaders and all our administration team to know what our numbers are because they're the ones who have the most influence over whether we succeed or not. I want them to know whether we're growing or shrinking; where we are succeeding or failing. I want them to know all our current strengths and weaknesses as a business because they can move the necessary levers that shift how we are running.

It's not always easy. It's straight-forward to be transparent when things are financially on track, but it's more difficult (even slightly embarrassing) when the business is struggling or when we are missing our targets. It's important to not convey insecurity or fear because if people don't know for sure their job will still be there next year, they may jump ship onto another business. So even while delivering tough financial news, it's important to exhibit optimism and outline the plans that the business has to get back on track.

**Transparency Invites Solutions**

Because we have been so transparent about our numbers and figures, we have been able to enjoy the feedback from all these staff on how to improve, and the insights from a group this large can be harnessed and put to great use helping us succeed in the future.

Also, when your team are invited to see the business' finances, they are more committed to helping the company grow and succeed.

**Keep Staff Salaries Confidential**

The only area of a healthy business where being financially transparent with staff can be dangerous is regarding people's salaries. It's vital that your staff is unaware of each other's salaries because as soon as they become public, people can easily become jealous of each other's larger pay rates and to "even the playing field" it can cost the business a lot of money. So wherever possible, ensure your staff do not have access or information on each other's pay rates.

**Being Real Works**

We're real about the numbers, and we're real about our successes and failures. It's part of having a healthy culture within our business. When everyone is on board with what the goal is, the company flourishes.

**Building Customer Perceptions of Your Business**

Customers know when a business feels like a healthy place to be, and over the medium term, they will come to see whether or not the company culture is on track.

You demonstrate to customers they can have confidence in you by clearly explaining what your purpose is, how you will serve them and by consistently delivering on the promises you make.

Whenever a new customer joins us, we let them know that the Big Improvements Tutoring team is here to serve and here to make a difference in the life of their child. We're here to reassure parents, to make their family life easier, and make life more comfortable for children at school. That's what we're all about. That's who we are. We're not here because we love the academic curriculum. We're not here because we're gung-ho about English, or super-passionate about maths. Instead, we are here because we love helping people.

What you stand for and the culture you're building needs to be conveyed effectively to your customers to give them confidence in your team.

## Consulting is Like Steroids

**DISCLAIMER**

Let's be real. I own and run a business consulting and business coaching group. It's called About To Fly, and it's at www.abouttofly.com. Frankly, I think most business consultants and coaches need to have a good, long hard look at themselves in the mirror and ask themselves why they can't give better results for the money they charge. Yes, I am biased and opinionated when it comes to discussing consulting and coaching, but that's largely because I am in the industry and I've seen enough to know what works and what is a waste of time and money.

**Choose Consulting over Coaching**

Consulting is when somebody comes into your business and shows you specific steps to take. Coaching is when someone is equipping you with the skills you need to deal with the issues you face in your own business. Both have a place, but for business growth to succeed at key, often challenging points, consulting will generally give you a bigger impact, bang for the buck. Nevertheless, there is value in both, and I pay for both consulting and coaching within my businesses. Great consulting works like steroids for your business in that it helps you grow faster than you could on your own.

### The 1.5% Consulting Rule

Here's something I am convinced of, yet I had to learn it the hard way. I've never come across it in a book before, but I wholeheartedly believe in it, and I'm building my next company on this advice, right from the start.

I believe that businesses should spend 1.5% of their revenue on business consulting - letting the best experts in the field show you exactly what your strategy should be and involving them in your business plans and practices. If you've got a $1 million annual turnover business, that's $15,000 each year. At $2 million, that's $30,000. A lot of people think "I can't spare that sort of money", but they don't realise they will spend it anyway on inefficient systems or practices if they don't pay an experienced consultant to help them decide on the right paths to follow.

### Consultants Solve Things for You

The right advice from a talented consultant will save you much more money in the long run than what you spend paying for their advice. Also, they will save you time because instead of finding yourselves "reinventing the wheel," a good, strategic consultant will show you the "right wheels" that are already out there waiting to be used.

**Consulting Pays for Itself**

One of the most important things we have done in the last couple of years was choosing to use a specialised business consultant who understood our industry. We paid him a lot of money, but he's paid for himself *four or five times over*. He was able to show us the blind spots we weren't aware of. When I was running a $1 million business, I had blind spots everywhere. At $2 million, I'm much more aware of the old blind spots, but with growth, new blind spots appear.

In the next year, my team will continue spending 1.5% of our revenue on consulting, hiring experts to look at our systems, procedures and strategies, and advising us about how we can improve them.

One day, when we're a $10 million business or a $100 million business, we will still be allocating 1.5%-to consulting because it really is a great investment.

When business owners believe they don't need an expert consultant, usually it just means their blind spots are well-hidden and their optimism and self-confidence are greater than warranted.

Also, great consulting work will always pay for itself. That's my biggest tip. If I had done this three or four years ago, we'd be twice the size we are now, and the growing pains would have been minimised.

Consultants Show You the Steps Forward

A consultant will help you map out the next steps to take on your growth journey. The best consultants will show you the small changes you can make to have a large impact on your business.

Avoid people who focus on issues that don't lead to better revenues or higher profits in the long-term.

A good consultant breaks bigger issues into smaller, bite-sized chunks. They help you deal with each little bite-sized chunk, and then offer you options for each area and maybe even help you implement your choice. That's good consulting.

From Whom Should You Get Advice?

You need to plan carefully and work out who is right to give you advice. Look for someone who has already successfully walked the path your business is on, who can step in from the outside and show you the hidden traps along the way.

You gain the most from someone who has seen identical or similar issues before, who can look at your strategy and see what things look like on the ground. Find someone who is happy to help you with implementing new ideas and policies, rather than someone who just tells you what to do. You need someone who will be hands-on and joining you in the 'trenches'.

Avoid "Theoretical" Consultants.

Beware of anyone who's going to be focused on looking at documentation and talking to you about documentation. That "intellectual" or "top-down" approach is way too theoretical, and it won't be likely to pay for itself. Most consultants with that approach haven't understood your business, or don't have enough business experience of their own, so instead of focusing on growing your profits they focus on plans. It's almost like they want to make a plan about how to make a plan, which is a poor use of time.

Instead, find someone who's going to come in and get involved in the action. They're going to sit in the office so they can see what happens day-to-day. They're going to go out to where you deliver your product or service to see what happens out there. They're going to look at your accounting figures, and they're going to sit down with you and work through everything.

**What Holds Businesses Back from the 1.5% Rule?**

Often business owners resist paying for consulting because when they were smaller, they had good mentors or friends who could help them with their business. The challenge is that as a company grows, there is a much higher level of expertise required to see what needs to be done next. Most business mentors haven't spent enough time in your business or even in your industry to be of great strategic help in the future when your scale is so much higher.

Another reason why so many people are hesitant to spend serious money on consulting is they fear paying someone without the right knowledge to give unqualified opinions. They imagine the consultant arriving, having a half-hearted look at their business, not fully understanding it, throwing out a lot of recommendations, and then dashing out the door leaving a huge invoice but no real results.

Avoid this scenario by choosing the right consultant and being clear on what they are going to deliver.

**A Guarantee Creates Certainty**

When I offer business coaching and consulting with About To Fly, I even put a guarantee on my work so that if people don't feel they receive great value from us, then they don't have to pay anything. However, I've never had someone take me up on that guarantee because I give great results they are happy with. Also, I've staked my reputation on the promise that we would pay for ourselves many times over by getting into the deeper, non-surface issues in businesses, finding the painful spots and then dealing with them. I know from my own experience that you don't need to solve everything in someone's business. You just need to find the pain points and the areas of greatest inefficiency and deal with them. Subsequently, the rest of the business will be easier to grow.

**Avoid Consultants Who are Overly-eager**

I once had a terrible experience with a consultant, and it cost our business a lot of wasted money. Unfortunately, I chose someone who had a broad knowledge of business, but who had never faced some of the industry-specific issues we faced. The big warning sign I had overlooked was that he was overly-eager to work for us.

Instead, I would have been better off finding someone who had a similar approach to About To Fly. That's because About To Fly doesn't work with just anybody.

Instead, we carefully select who we will and won't work for. We have no interest in trying to support businesses that we don't have the background skills or knowledge to help. I would rather say "No" to a potential client and direct them elsewhere than try to support a client whose needs don't match our skill set.

Unfortunately, not everyone takes this approach so choose wisely.

**Surprising Ourselves**

If someone had told me two years ago about the 1.5% rule I wouldn't have realised its value. Also, if they'd predicted that today I would now be spending 1.5% of my revenue on consulting, I wouldn't have believed them. However, I can't argue with measurable results, especially financial results. It's clear to me that good consulting pays for itself in my businesses. So, I suggest businesses avoid fumbling around, continuing to make the same preventable mistakes. Get good consulting, plant that "seed money", and watch your business grow.

*Do you need a hand?*

*I help business owners just like you to get the best profits and lifestyle from their businesses.*

*To get some real help or to learn how you can grow your business into something you'll love,* get in touch with me at:

    www.abouttofly.com

## Smart Growth Planning

Growth is a double-edged sword. Growth in revenue or profits can only come with more work in system-building, problems, stress, hard work and challenges. Growth is like a drug that business owners become easily addicted to, but the side-effects of growth done badly are debilitating.

**Beware of Foolish Growth**

Recently I was reading about someone whose business goal was to have the capacity to service a million customers, and they were halfway to their goal. I looked at that goal and thought, "That's a stupid goal - clearly their egos are larger than their brains."

Understand me correctly here - it's not stupid that they want to grow. What's stupid is that their objective is all about revenue and reach. Their eyes are on how many customers they're going to have. How foolish - because if they reach their goal, but lack sustainable, reliable profitability then they have pursued a goal that is counter-productive in the long-term! Instead, their goal would be healthier if it was focused on the profitability of their existing customers. Alternatively, setting the goal of having a million customers would be appropriate as long as it comes at a minimum level of profitability that could be tied into that goal.

It's great to add new customers, but only if the profit margin stays healthy. Growth without profitability is always going to have devastating consequences. With growth comes drama. If you're going to grow, the profitability needs to be there to justify the extra work that growth generates.

## Guard Your Profit Margins

When you first started working for yourself, you probably had very high margins that gradually came down as you employed others and scaled. In the next year or two, when you're going from $1 million to $2 million, you must focus on pushing that profitability margin back up. It's hard to find many very large companies with a large profit margin. So evaluate, is the growth you're seeking worth it? Make sure you understand the profit you expect to make from doing so and analyse whether or not it's worth it. Growth simply for the sake of growth can be very destructive.

## Beware of Losing your Niche

If you want to turn your $1 million turnover business into a $2 million turnover business, you need to plan for how you're going to grow. It's not going to happen by itself!

There are a couple of ways you can grow, but you need to resist the strong temptation to step out of your niche. Do not diversify into areas that are not your niche. Otherwise, as you grow, you can lose your "specialness" and become just like other businesses in your industry. So growth is important, but choosing the right way of growing is even more important.

**What is Your Growth Plan?**

There are many ways your business could grow, but here are the most likely ways:

- Super-enhanced marketing to add more customers;
- Adding new locations to expand your geographical reach;
- Adding extra services or products to your offering;
- Partnering with another business to sell through their channels;
- Purchasing a similar business to assimilate into yours;
- Inviting an investor to fund your growth.

**Super-enhanced Marketing to Add More Customers**

The easiest and most straightforward way to grow is to super-enhance your marketing. It's important to distinguish super-enhancing from simply "improving" your marketing. Here's the difference - many businesses can improve their marketing and make a small impact on how effectively they grow their new customer base. But that is a very small thing compared to super-enhancing your marketing by adding 100%, 200% or even 400% to your marketing budget and finding brand-new, far more effective ways of letting potential customers know you exist and have the best solutions for meeting their needs.

Super-enhancing your marketing may mean using an entirely new channel of marketing, such as starting a massive Google Ad campaign, a regular magazine "info-marketing" column in a niche magazine, or even creating a brand-new magazine for your industry.

Before you "bet the farm" on a plan for super-enhancing your marketing, definitely run some small-scale experiments to test whether or not your chosen strategy is likely to work. Never put big money into something until you have tested its benefits on a smaller scale. For marketing (and most things in business), remember that playing by the "Minimum Viable Product" philosophy protects you from wasting your marketing money.

Also, if you are going to spend big dollars to play in the leagues of the big businesses, understand that you will be out of your depth the moment you start. That's why you need to hire talented, experienced experts to create and run your marketing for you. Even if you believe you are strong at marketing, it is usually more effective and cost-effective to let experts lead your business here.

If you can make this work, it is a very effective way of growing your business and it is the strategy that I recommend for most businesses I work with.

## Add New Locations to Expand Your Geographical Reach

Is it possible to grow your business by taking what works in your current location and "copying and pasting" that into a second location to give you access to more people?

For example, if you have a highly successful business, you may be able to create another outlet on the other side of your city, or even in another city.

There are significant financial risks with starting new locations. Be aware of the large set-up costs, plan carefully, and get great advice before you pursue this style of growth. If your business model is healthy, it can be terrific for you, but to go ahead and do this without a proven business model or without healthy profit margins will be likely to hurt or kill your business.

Also pursuing this means of growth requires you to create new systems to keep your end-product quality high while someone else delivers it.

## Add Extra Services or Products to Your Offering

Will you add extra services that are fine-tuned to what your current customers are looking for? For example, a successful vet could start a dog-training school on weekends or a garden maintenance business could "branch out" into offering tree-cutting. Usually, a business can explore these options in a carefully measured way, using small-scale experiments that won't do long-term financial damage if things don't work out.

**Partner with Another Business to Sell through their Channels.**

This is a very risky strategy because when you partner with another business, you are willingly choosing to put your future in their hands. Remember that other businesses will always prioritise their own future over yours, so if you do find a way to work with another business, then keep this as a small growth channel and keep all your other options open because the day will almost certainly come when the arrangement comes to an end. Examples of doing this would be to set up a wholesaling arrangement or for an accounting business to partner with a business coach to cross-refer work to each other for a fee. These arrangements can work, but they are risky, hard to control, and are unreliable ways of growing.

**Buying a Business for Growth**

Now for a word of warning. At your scale of business, you're getting to the stage where you may consider looking at acquisitions - buying other businesses to "bolt on" to your own business or buying other businesses to absorb into your own culture. I've done that, and it nearly sent us broke.

When you buy a business, you are buying something that is very difficult to change because that business' customers and staff will resist changes every step of the way. Challenges that should be straightforward to solve are always harder when it isn't a business you already have the leadership of and cultural influence over.

I learned the hard way how financially destructive and stressful it is to buy an existing business. I bought a business from a great friend whose company I had been involved in as a consultant for a few years. Imagine how much harder it is to buy from a stranger or to purchase a business that you've never worked in!

When you try to absorb another business into your own, the new business brings with it all its unresolved dramas and all their half-built systems that are incompatible with your own. Good luck with that!

Their staff has a different mindset, different motivations, a different purpose, and will be primarily focused on keeping their jobs. Their customers are going to come to you with different expectations about what you will do for them.

These are some of the reasons why most business acquisitions do not deliver what the new owners were hoping for.

Acquisitions are tough. I'm not saying don't ever buy someone else's business but if you do then go ahead with an accurate understanding of how significant (and potentially draining) the challenge ahead of you will be.

**Beware of Inviting Investors to Fund Your Growth**

You need to be able to fund your growth, but this isn't a safe way to do it. A lot of business owners spend a lot of time talking about how to persuade others to buy in and invest in your business. This is very dangerous because investors want to make a quick profit, which usually requires some risky or reckless strategy.

Remember, if your business isn't generating enough profit to fund its own growth, you really shouldn't be thinking about expansion. Instead, you would be financially better off by dealing with the underlying profitability issues or shutting the business down. Growth should be organic; it should be internal. It shouldn't come from a wealthy investor riding on a white horse coming to rescue you.

The accidentally good news for most business owners who want to pursue the strategy of finding an outside investor is that very few outside investors are interested in buying a business that isn't already thriving. Luckily, that has prevented many mediocre businesses from tying themselves to an investor, despite their own best efforts.

Also, keep in mind that once you have an investor in your business, you've lost the autonomy that has brought you this far and created a partnership you'll be tied to in the longer term. It's the business equivalent of "marrying for money," and it is not a recipe for long term joy.

## Upgrade Your Systems in Preparation for Growth

If you're going to grow, you're going to need better-built systems and practices to keep up with the new workload. You will probably need new software or even some custom-built software. Despite these sorts of investments, you're going to need to keep your profitability high by changing your current workflow to deal with the bottlenecks and the inefficiencies of your business.

Growth looks glamorous, but it's a long journey. Experienced business owners keep a realistic perspective on growth, asking proactive questions:

- How do we keep our profit margins healthy?
- What support structures and systems do we need?
- How do we make sure we have the right people and a consistently healthy culture?
- How do we continuously and cost-effectively increase our marketing?
- Is there still a large, untapped market within our niche, or have we already come close to saturating that market?

**Strategic Errors During Growth are Extra Dangerous**

You can make a significant strategic mistake when you're a half-million dollar business and although it will be painful, your business will most likely survive and learn from it. However, a similar mistake when you're a $2 million business could mean the end for you. Game over. Mistakes at a larger scale are harder to bounce back from. So, be careful and ensure you have a sensible, well-tested, well-planned strategy about how you're going to grow.

**Despite All the Risks, You must Grow**

Clearly, there are many dangers and risks to the health and sustainability of your business while you grow. Despite the challenges, it's also vital to recognise a business that isn't growing is probably going backwards. Therefore, your business does need to grow.

The sobering warnings you have read in this chapter are not there to scare you away from future growth. They are simply there to mark some of the danger zones on the path ahead of you so you can have the best chance of succeeding.

You always want to be growing, and when you are growing, stay focused on the important growth ingredients such as efficient systems, high-profit margins, and the cultural health of your company. So, go for growth, but grow wisely and with a strategy that will work.

**Great Growth is Worth Fighting For**

There is something special and exhilarating about running a company that is growing. The confidence among your staff when they know they are part of a winning team is tremendous. Terrific growth is challenging but well worth fighting for. Growth isn't safe, but it is the fuel for the real adventure and joy of running a business.

## Your "Freedom Tasks" for Big Results

Right now, grab a pen and a piece of paper and start scribbling. I know it's an effort to get off the couch and reach for it, but in a few quick, easy minutes, you will have new insights on how you want to prioritise your work time. It will be worth it! After you've done the two "freedom tasks" I'm giving you, you will experience a lot more clarity about what your next moves are at work. It's liberating, and worth the energy, so keep that pen and paper handy.

### Freedom Task #1: Five Minutes of Prioritising

I dare you to take this mini-game on and see how you can put it to use in your own business. It's made a massive difference for me, so I'm keen to suggest it to others. Now, get ready to jot down some insights into how you can reduce your working hours.

Do you remember the Pareto Principle, also known as the 80/20 rule)? 20% of your efforts produce 80% of your results.

I'm guessing that you probably work about 50 hours each week, so 20% of that is 12 hours.

Let's imagine you could only work for 12 hours a week for the next 12 months. I know it sounds crazy, but let's imagine that you contracted some strange unheard-of disease that capped your working ability to a maximum of 12 hours per week. In that sort of situation, there are 10 questions you need to ask yourself to work out how your business would survive (and hopefully thrive) – so write down your answers:

1. How would you spend your 12 hours of weekly work time?
2. What tasks and what systems would you put your heart and soul into building for those 12 hours?
3. What meetings would you stop going to?
4. What projects have you been putting time into but still aren't achieving real results and would need to be dropped? (What projects really need to be cut out of your business and your life?)
5. What tasks would you need to delegate?
6. What would you need to stop doing altogether?
7. Which staff members are not adding value to your team, and need to go?
8. Which annoying, needy, time-consuming customers would you need to stop paying close attention to (and be willing to lose

them)?
9. Whom would you put in charge of your current workload?
10. How would you choose to spend the 38 spare hours each week having fun? (You know - the time that you had cut out of your work-week?)

That's a lot to think about, but you'll get some ideas going in under ten minutes. This will give you clarity on where you should be focusing your attention, and it will let you get on with it. The 12-hour work week is about "snip, snip, snipping away" all the excess things that don't add real value to your business.

Also, I dare you to try one 12-hour work week. See what happens. What could you lose, right? It's as easy as grabbing your work diary and choosing a week within the next 2-4 weeks and set aside some big chunks of time for yourself or your family.

I've done it, and it is soooooo liberating! You'll soon realise "I don't need to do all these extra tasks I've been forcing myself to do. My staff are more competent than I thought. My processes work better than I thought, and now I've realised that I don't need to micromanage things so much!"

Don't get me wrong - I'm not doing a 12-hour work week every week, but I love to do it sometimes, and it feels great! It not only lets you focus, but it also gives you clarity of purpose. It's how life would be if you were acting as a true "business owner" instead of a "slave to your business."

**Freedom Task #2: Three Minutes of Prioritising Relationships**

Now, while you've still got your pen in hand, here is a 3-minute task that helps you get perspective on your most important business relationships. This time it's just five questions, so go ahead and jot down your answers to uncover some hidden assets you may have overlooked.

1. Who are your best mentors - the people who help you grow your skills and abilities the most?
2. Who are you looking to for advice? When things seem unwinnable, to whom do you turn?
3. Who's on your support team—those who "have your back" no matter what you face?
4. Who's helping you plan and strategise to grow your business to the next level?
5. Which members of your team have hidden talents or super-skills that are currently being wasted, but could be tapped into to make a big difference in your business?

Well done. What did you discover? Who do you need to send an email text message or phone call to right now to set up a coffee with?

## Freedom Tasks Lead to Clarity

That was certainly worth doing. It's likely you've got some you clarity on a few areas of your business and on some relationships. Remember that clarity without action does not create change, but taking actions is what generates long-term, lasting results. Make it happen.

## A Personal Invitation from Michael

Congratulations!

You have my personal respect because you have read through some of the toughest sections of this book and you have hung in there. You are clearly committed to growing your business and getting your life back. That puts you in the 10% of business owners who are willing to make real changes in their business, instead of the 90% who "talk the talk" but don't "walk the walk."

That's why I'd love to invite you to come and get some more value from my "profitability lab"—About To Fly. It's easy—just go to [www.abouttofly.com](www.abouttofly.com) to book your FREE 20-minute strategy session. Coming up with the right strategy will lead you to real results. Your session might be with me, or I might introduce you to another member of my team (depending on what your business actually needs).

You'll notice that I didn't tell people about this invitation to a "strategy session" in the early chapters of the book. That's because I only want to work with people who are committed and who have "stickability" in their character.

So, what have you got to lose? How could you pass up an invitation like that?

Let's make some positive changes happen

before you even continue to the next chapter. Jump on my website and take a minute to contact me there:

www.abouttofly.com

# You've Got This! Go Make it Happen!

## Play Smarter, not Harder

I hope you've got a whole stack of insights about turning your $1 million business to a $2 million business. It's a big task ahead, but a journey of a thousand miles starts with a few steps, so go for it!

You don't have to learn the hard way. I mentioned before that one of the things that led me to write this was finding myself in the back of an ambulance because I had worked myself too hard, frantically pursuing too many goals at once. My business had grown, but my skills to run it had not. Grow your skills.

## Valuable Wake-up Call

Let's be clear - the back of an ambulance is a scary place to be. It's also pretty intimidating being in a hospital with technicians giving you brain scans because the doctor wants to assess whether or not you've had a stroke.

For the next six weeks, I lived my life thinking that if the medication didn't do its job, I could drop dead at any moment.

That was the wakeup call life gave me - "Wake up and change what you're doing in your business!"

It was six weeks later that I finally felt relieved. It was finally time for my appointment with a neurologist (brain specialist) who told me all I had experienced was a really bad migraine, with some pretty weird side-effects that fooled the other doctors into believing I'd suffered a stroke. Thank goodness all the assessments had clearly shown I hadn't had a stroke at all and I was 'in the clear'.

It was a tough experience, but it was the wake-up call I needed. I hope you can learn without something that serious happening in your life.

**Good Luck on Your Journey**

I hope you got a lot of helpful strategic advice out of this book. Even if you only put some of the strategies you have read into place, you can expect to make much healthier profits and reduce your work hours by a lot. I encourage you to give it your best and to enjoy your work.

Unlike most business owners, I hope you will put sensible boundaries around your work, so your personal life and family life stays on track while your business grows. Go out there and make a difference in the world because your business really can do that. Also, always remember why you got into business in the first place, and truly live as an owner of your business, not as a slave to it.

Enjoy your growth towards becoming a $2 million company. If there's anything I can do to help you out, feel free to get in touch with me at www.abouttofly.com

because I actually read every email that readers of my books send to me (I figure if you take the time to reach out to me, I want to take the time for you, too).

## Final Tip: The Golden Rule of Business

I couldn't help but remind you of the golden rule of business – "Look after others in the way that you would want them to look after you."

It works with staff, customers and even your family. (I've been told it doesn't always work with in-laws, but you won't know unless you try, right?)

I hope my book has been my way of looking after you and making a contribution to your life (not just your business). I hope that aside from helping your business profits grow, it also helps you relax a bit on your business journey and enjoy it more.

Could I please ask you to take 2 minutes out of your day, and write a review of this book so others can find out about it? 5-star reviews are super-powerful for letting the Amazon "algorithm" know that it should show this book to others who are searching for help.

I think it's a great opportunity for you to be able to immediately apply the golden rule of business.

I encourage you to return to Amazon.com where you downloaded this book and leave a review:

Have you seen my other book that is specifically for business owners who have a fast-paced business?

It's titled *You're a Business Owner, Not a Slave*, and you can buy it here:

https://www.amazon.com/dp/B07KPQLMLY

On the following pages are samples of this book to get you started—my favourites:

## How to Increase Profitability

On the road to being a success both at work and at home, certain things have to be bedrock foundations for you. You have to get these things right. First off, and most importantly, you have to be making a healthy profit. Your business has to be succeeding financially. If your business is not making a decent amount of profit and you've been working on it for three years or more, you should seriously consider whether or not it's worth continuing. Think of your opportunities you are giving up in order to stay in your business. After all, you could get a regular job somewhere and earn a reliable wage without all the responsibility and stress you currently carry. Don't find yourself holding onto a non-profitable business just because you have pinned your ego or reputation to it. Either make your business nicely profitable or drop it.

Most businesses are run by people who do not make the important distinction between revenue and profit. Revenue is the money that comes into your bank account. Profits are what you keep at the end of the month. You need to objectively evaluate the likelihood of your business succeeding in the long term, and you do that by looking at the profit, not the revenue. To make things succeed at work, you must be profitable. If you're not making enough that your gross profit margins are at least 10% (sustainably healthy) or better yet 15% (very healthy), then something's broken. You need to be willing to face that because, without those sorts of margins, you will struggle to survive the next downturn that will inevitably come your way. Also, without a reasonable profit margin, your business will lack the budget to get to the point where it can do well without your constant, watchful eye over it.

I'm not asking you to do something I haven't already done because I have made a lot of very hard decisions in my business in the last year or two that meant we lost a lot of clients but made much higher profits. Everyone around me knows these are decisions I absolutely didn't want to make. Yet the irony is that the very same, difficult decisions that were hard on my conscience, and initially caused me a lot of self-doubt and fear were the path that led to my business becoming healthy, profitable and making a substantial income. I've learned from experience that it is less painful to make a tough decision than it is to delay committing to a course of action. My wife used to regularly tell me, "Oh, you look so stressed." She doesn't say that as often anymore because I know things are very much on track at work. We've now got a steady profit coming in each month, and we have plenty of time to relax and enjoy it. Profit is an antidote to stress and fear.

Now if you're sitting there thinking, "It's impossible to quickly turn around my profitability with just a few moves," hold that thought. I'll bet that you can. Here are some things I've done in the last year which helped me do just that, and maybe you can take similar steps.

**Increase Your Prices**

(Face your fear that all your customers will run away)

I've increased my prices because if I can't make a good profit now, I'm not interested in growing my business at low margins. I can't think of many things more stressful than that. I deliver a fantastic experience for my customers, and I deserve to make a profit. My wife and children deserve to reap the financial benefits that come from the hours I have taken from them and put into our business. Every time we've increased our prices, I've feared we would lose enormous numbers of our customers, but each time, I've been pleasantly surprised when most of our customers have stayed with us. Even when you do lose some customers while raising your prices, you can expect to make higher profits overall because the customers you keep will generate more profits for you, and you will have reduced your cost-base by no longer needing to serve those lost customers."

The excerpt from *You're a Business Owner, Not a Slave* ends here…If you like what you just read, you can buy it here:

https://www.amazon.com/dp/B07KP9LMLY

## Are You Ready to Grow the Next Level?

Talk to me – I'm a real person

I'd accomplished what I'd set out to do in my tutoring business, and it hums along nicely which has freed up a lot of time for me to pursue my other passions. So now I work with business owners just like you to help them increase their profitability and get their free time back. I created About To Fly as a strategic business coaching experience for entrepreneurs and business owners.

What makes About To Fly different from every other consulting group is that I help business owners break free from the stranglehold their business has over their time and their lives. Do you see why that's so important?

I have different ways of helping businesses of almost any size. Whatever your business size is, there are always ways I can help you make more money, work a whole lot less, and enjoy your life a whole lot more.

Your perseverance and commitment to find, buy, and finish reading a book like this reflects your "can-do" attitude and rock-solid character as a business owner.

Just for you—because you made it to the end of the book and journeyed through some challenging issues and a bit of soul searching — here's a secret...

Tell me when you send a message that "I read the full book". If you do that, I've got something extra special for you to ensure you get my absolute best strategic help.

So take action now—get some extra value from About To Fly. It's easy—just go to [www.abouttofly.com](http://www.abouttofly.com) to book a FREE 20-minute strategy session

## About the Author

Michael Guy Clark's unconventional business strategies are simultaneously loved by practical business-owners and hated by academic-types who don't think "outside the box." After an adventurous career in teaching school, he built and now runs Big Improvements Tutoring which disrupted the industry in two major cities and now helps kids in ten locations.

He also created About To Fly which is a unique business profitability lab, supporting niche businesses in tough industries.

If a genie would grant him one wish for his clients and other business owners, it would ask that it be to give them the knowledge of how to structure their business to run effectively and profitably without the owners' constant input. Due to the lack of genies, he wrote this book to help instead.

Michael enjoys bike-riding with his fun-loving wife and jumping on the trampoline with his two energetic kids.

## How to Order

**You may order this book direct from Amazon.com at:**
https://www.amazon.com/dp/B07KPBM1XJ

## Contact Information

I'm a real person, and just like you, I check my emails each day. I love to be surprised by feedback from former clients or people like you who read my books and get something out of them. I'll do my best to respond within a few days. If you take the time to reach out, I'll take the time to reply.

## Michael@abouttofly.com

## Amazon.com

https://www.amazon.com/dp/B07KPBM1XJ

If you purchased *Surprising Business Growth Secrets* from Amazon.com or have an Amazon.com account, please go there and give this book a rating of up to five stars. I'd also love for you to go ahead and leave a review (takes 2 minutes). This is a big help to me and also is great for helping the right readers discover these books.

www.ingramcontent.com/pod-product-compliance
Lightning Source LLC
Chambersburg PA
CBHW020433220526
45464CB00002B/679